Big Cocks Coloring Book for Adults

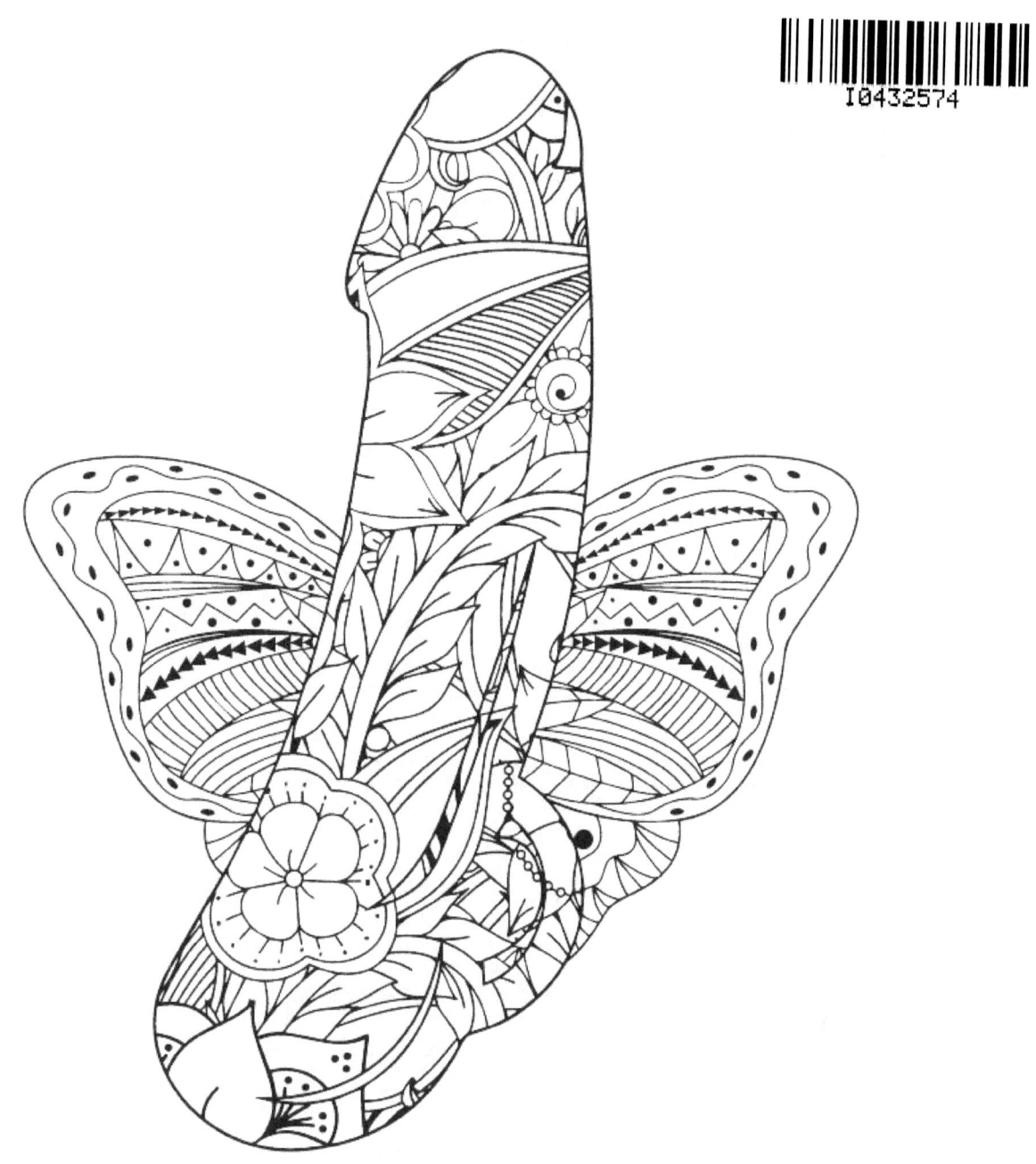

Over 30 Penis & Dick Inspired Dirty, Naughty Coloring Pages With Floral, Paisley, Mandala & Doodle Designs for Stress Relief & Relaxation

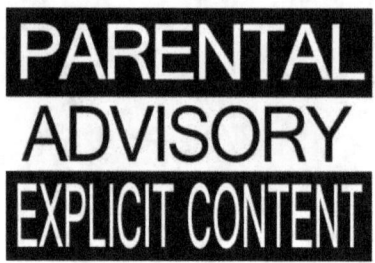

Copyright © 2017 Dirty Coloring Books For Adults. All rights reserved.
No part of this book may be reproduced or transmitted in any form by any means,
electronic or mechanical, including photocopying, scanning and recording,
or by any information storage and retrieval system,
without permission in writing from the publisher,
except for the review for inclusion in a magazine, newspaper or broadcast.

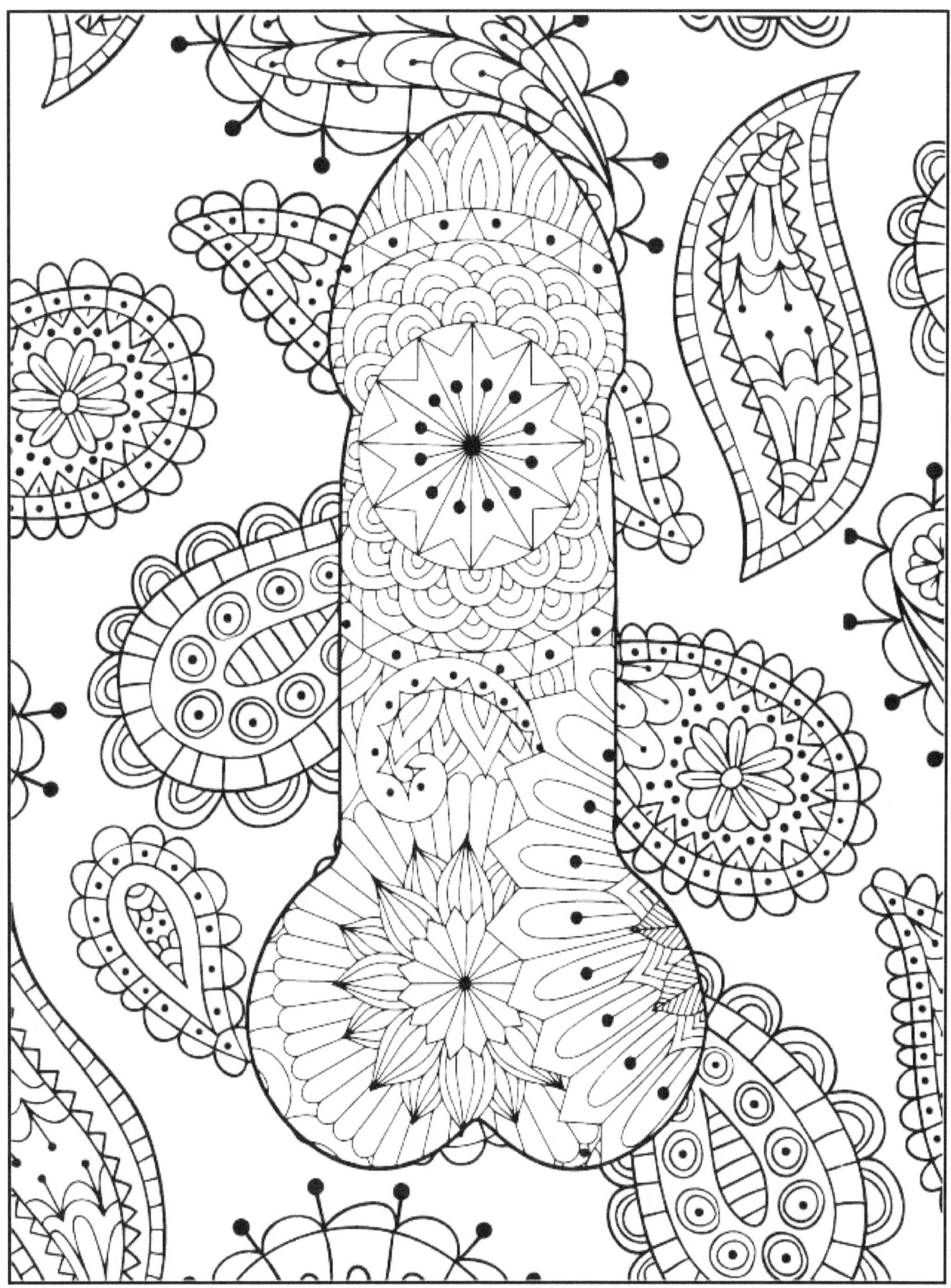

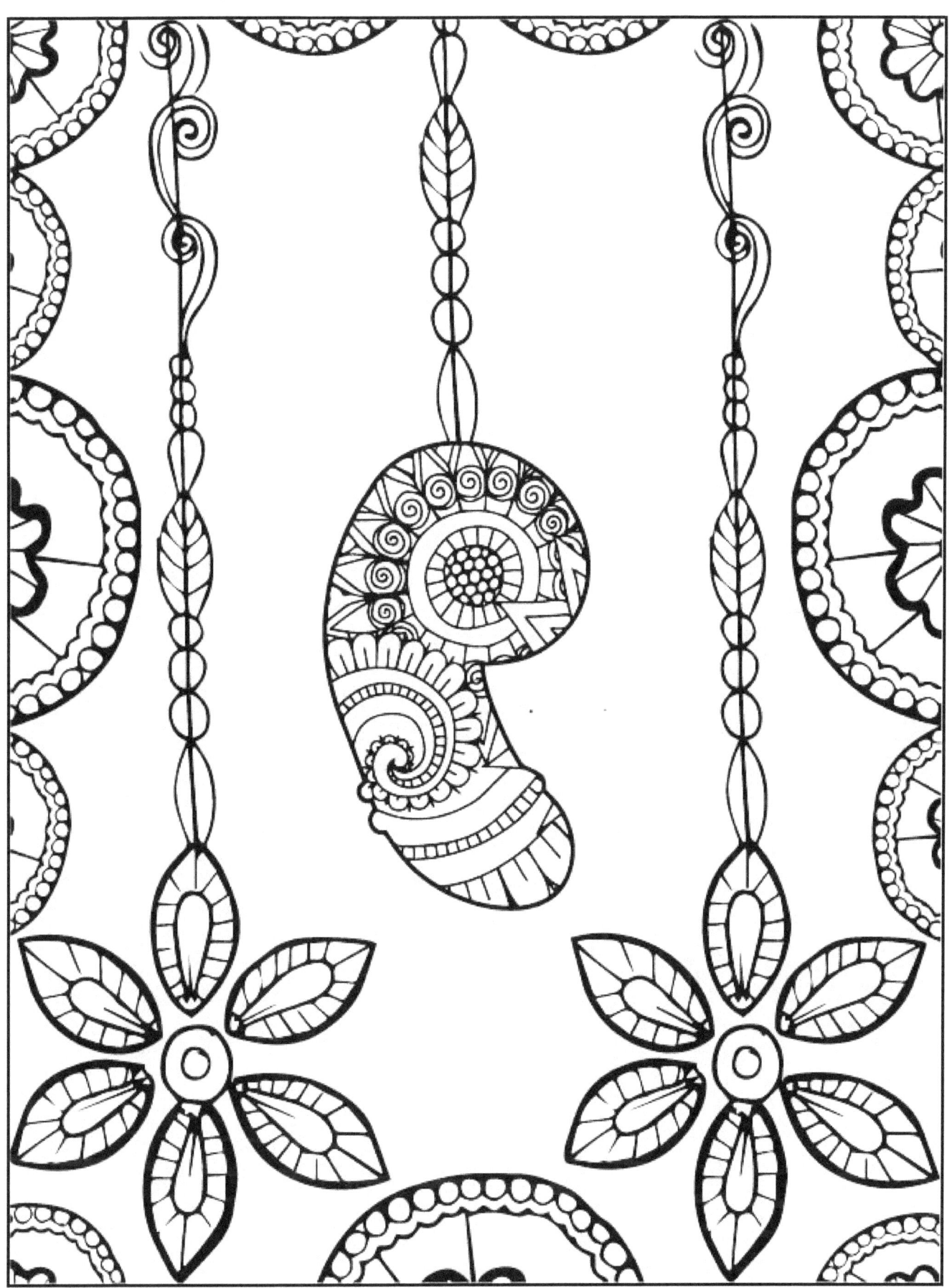

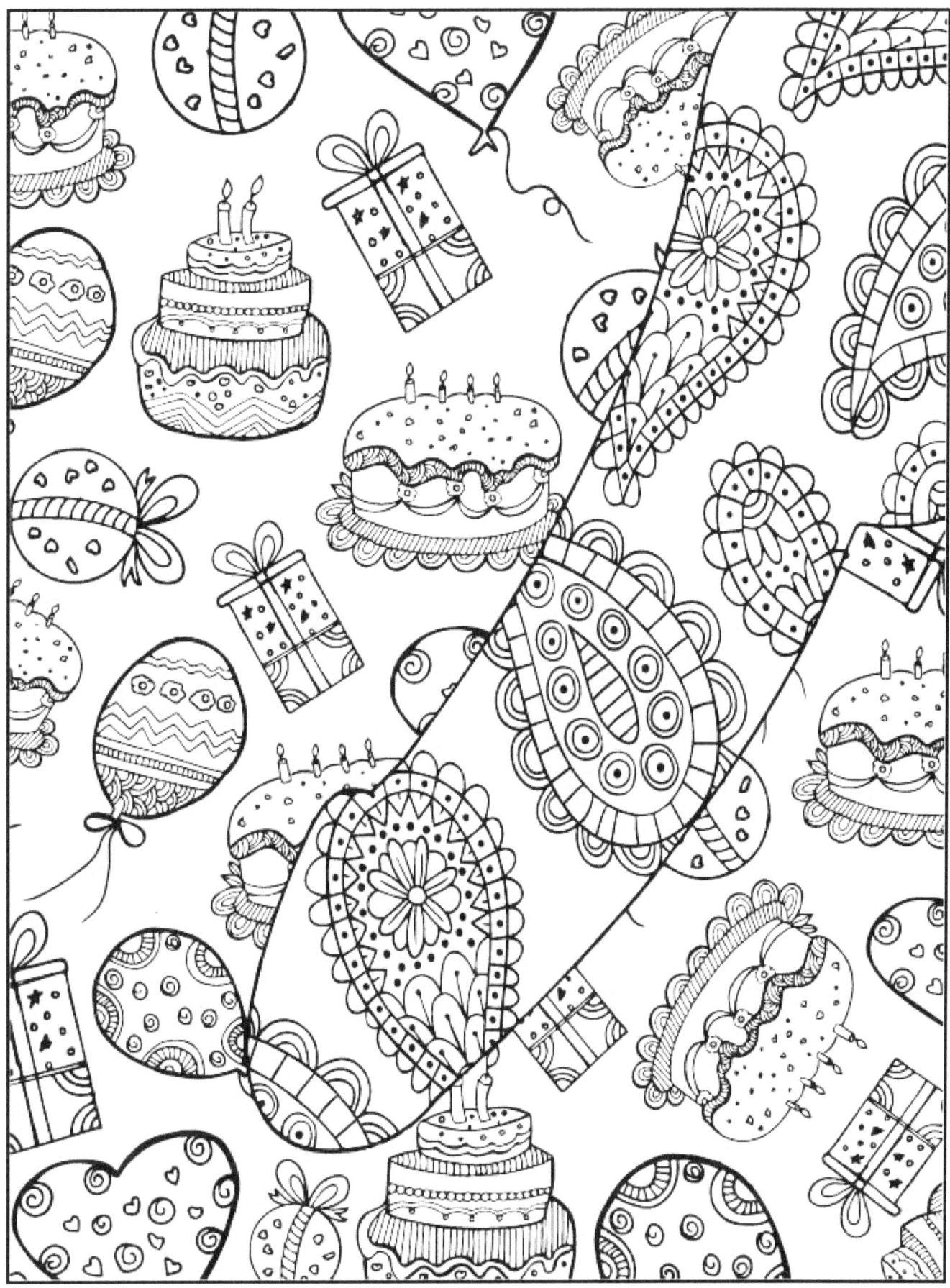

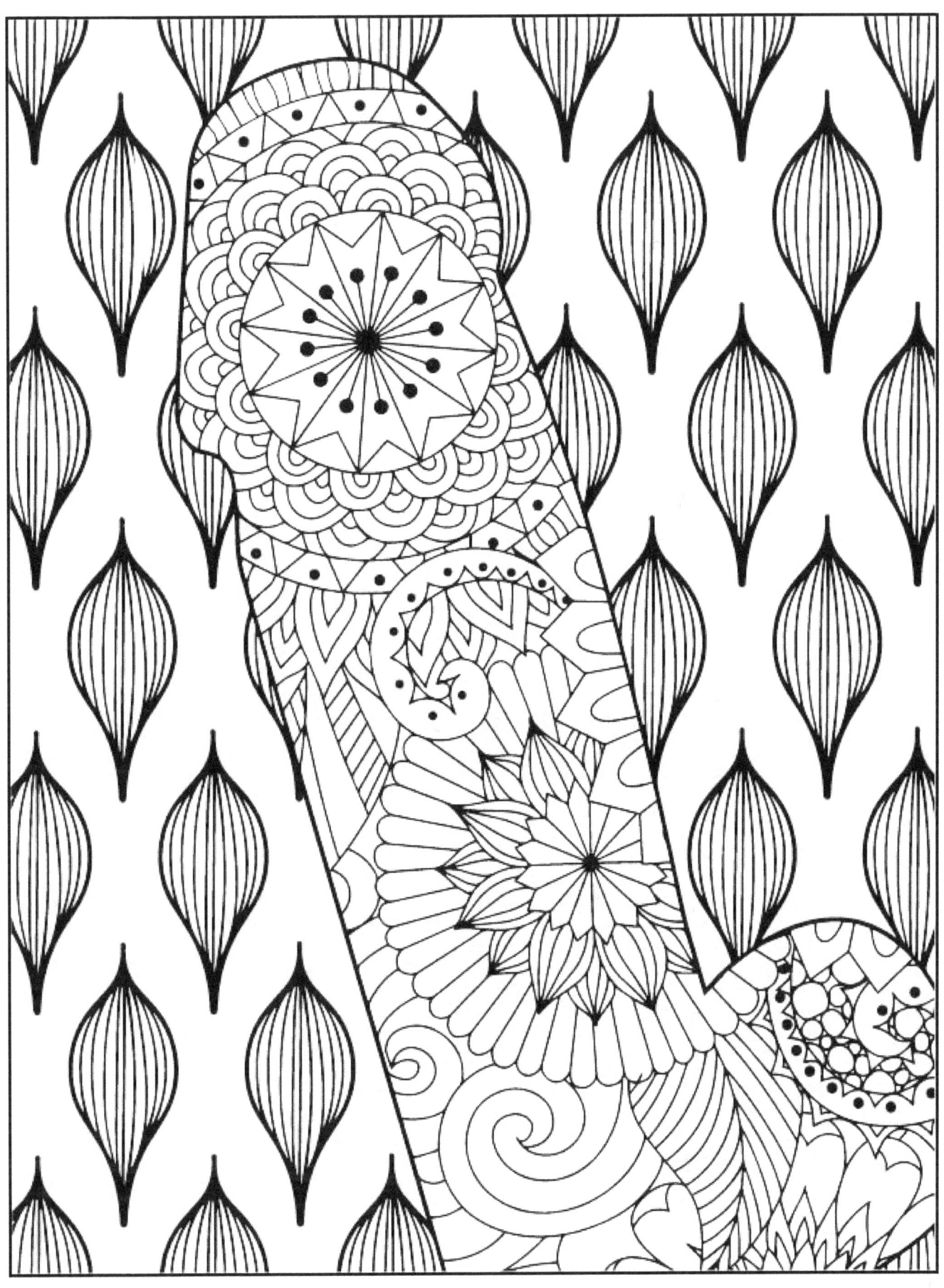

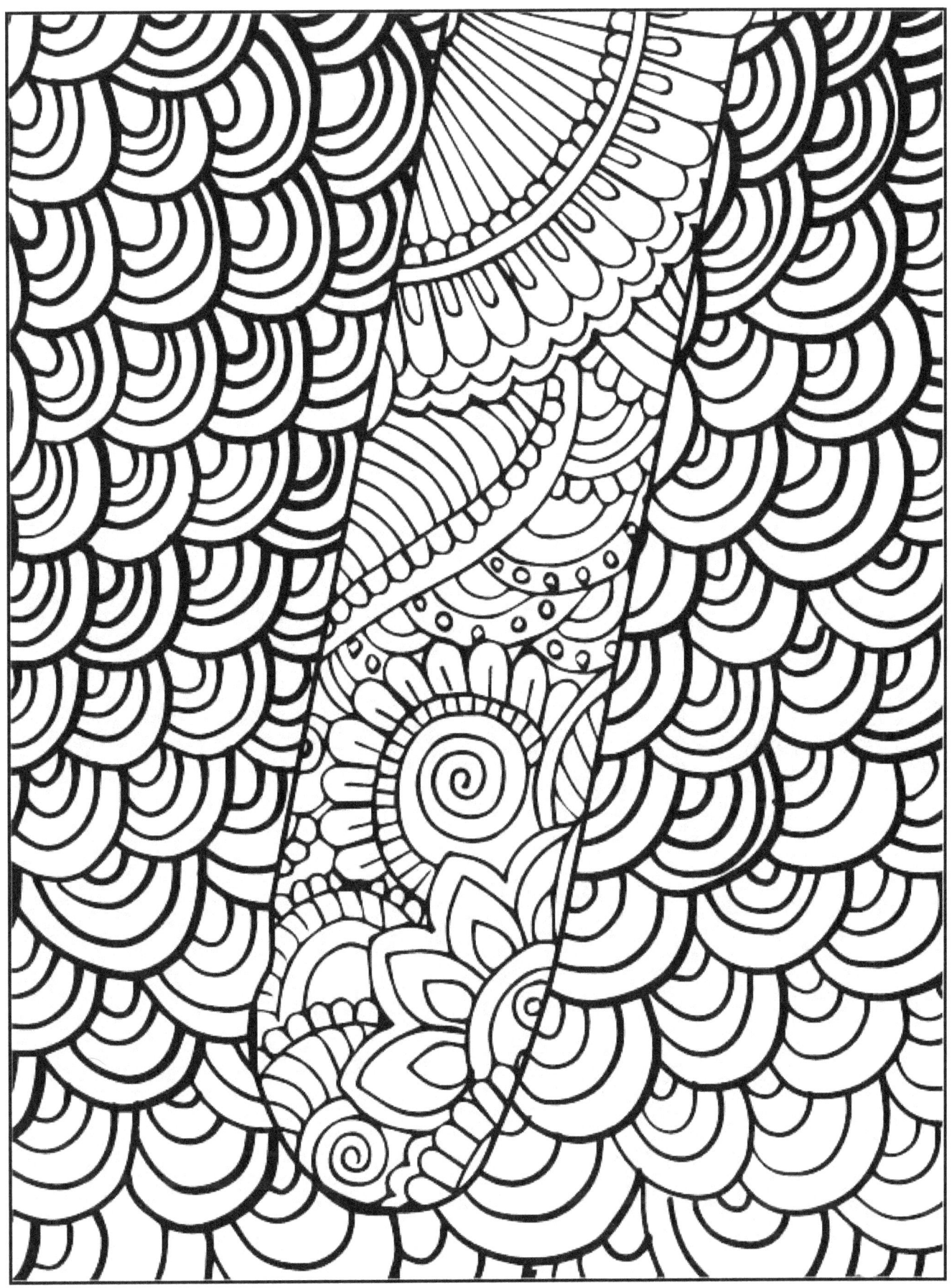

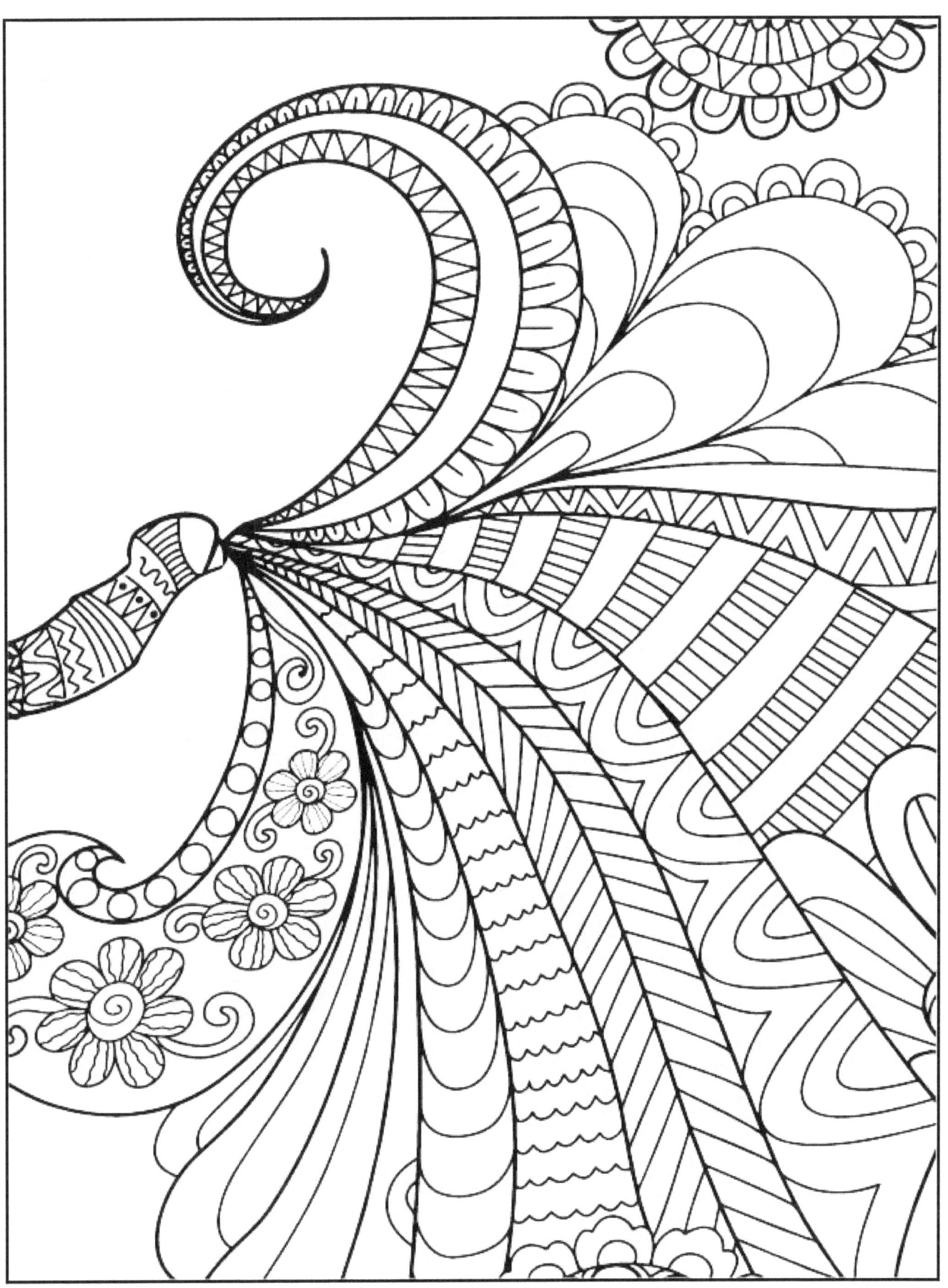

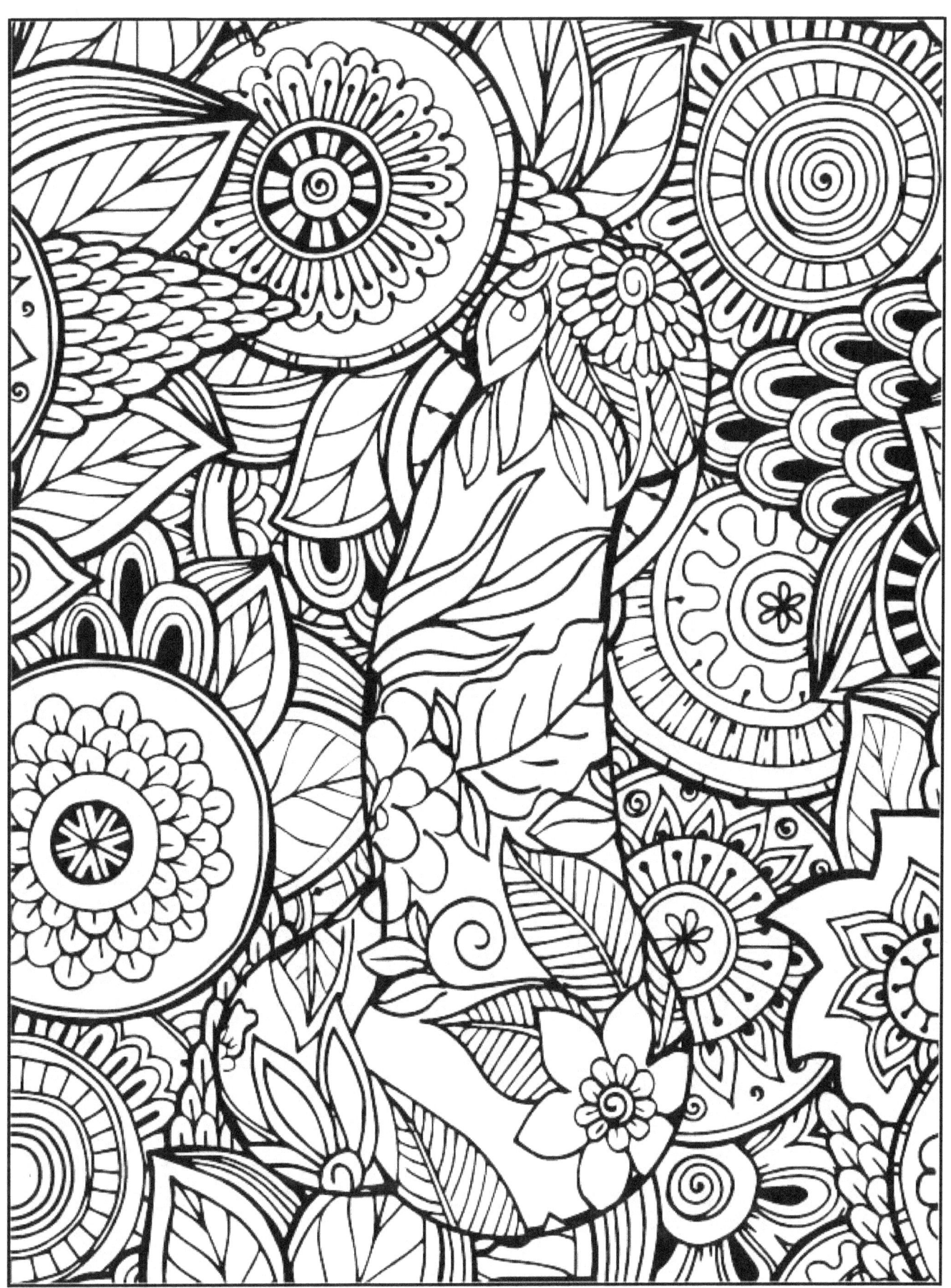

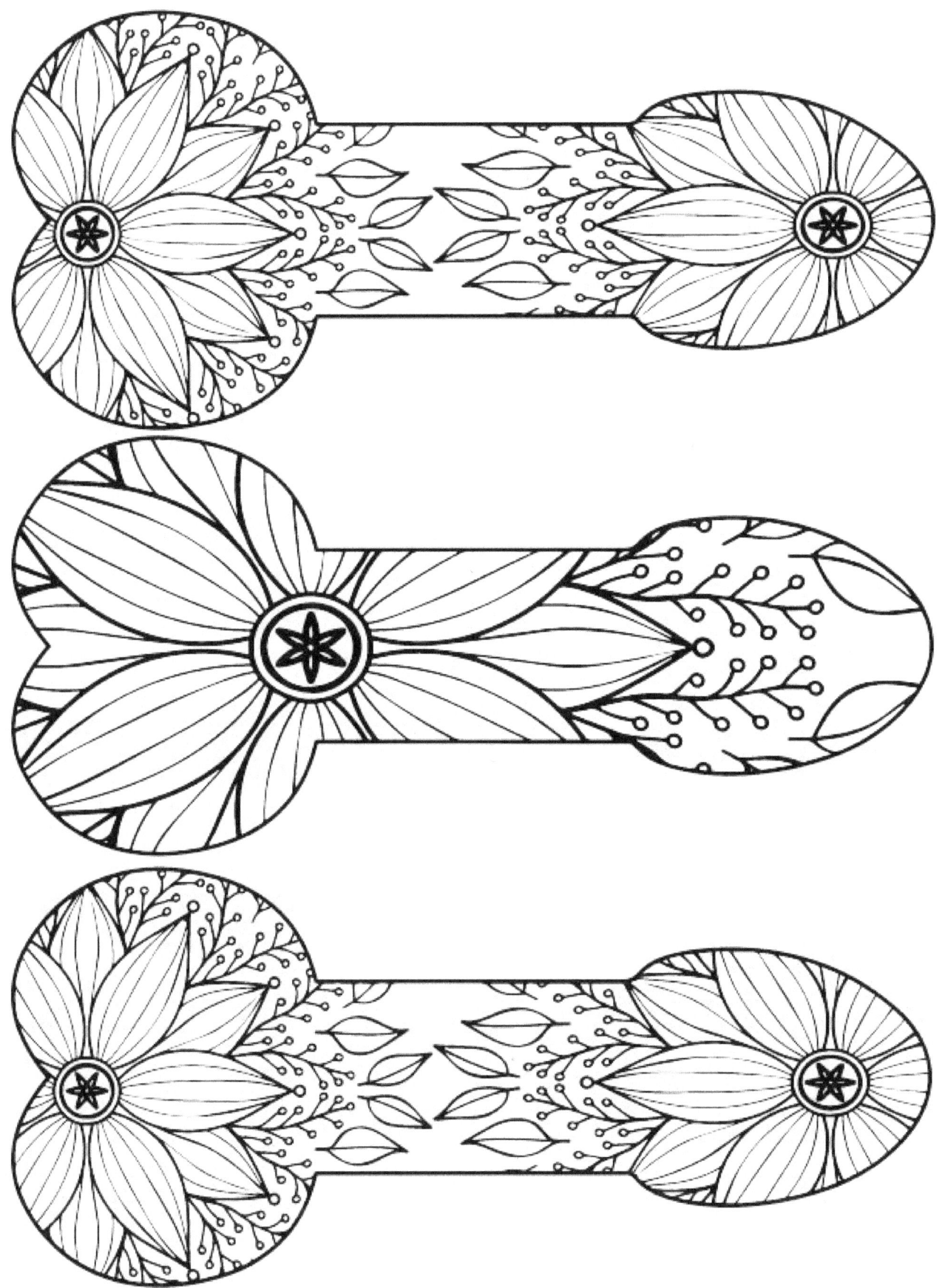

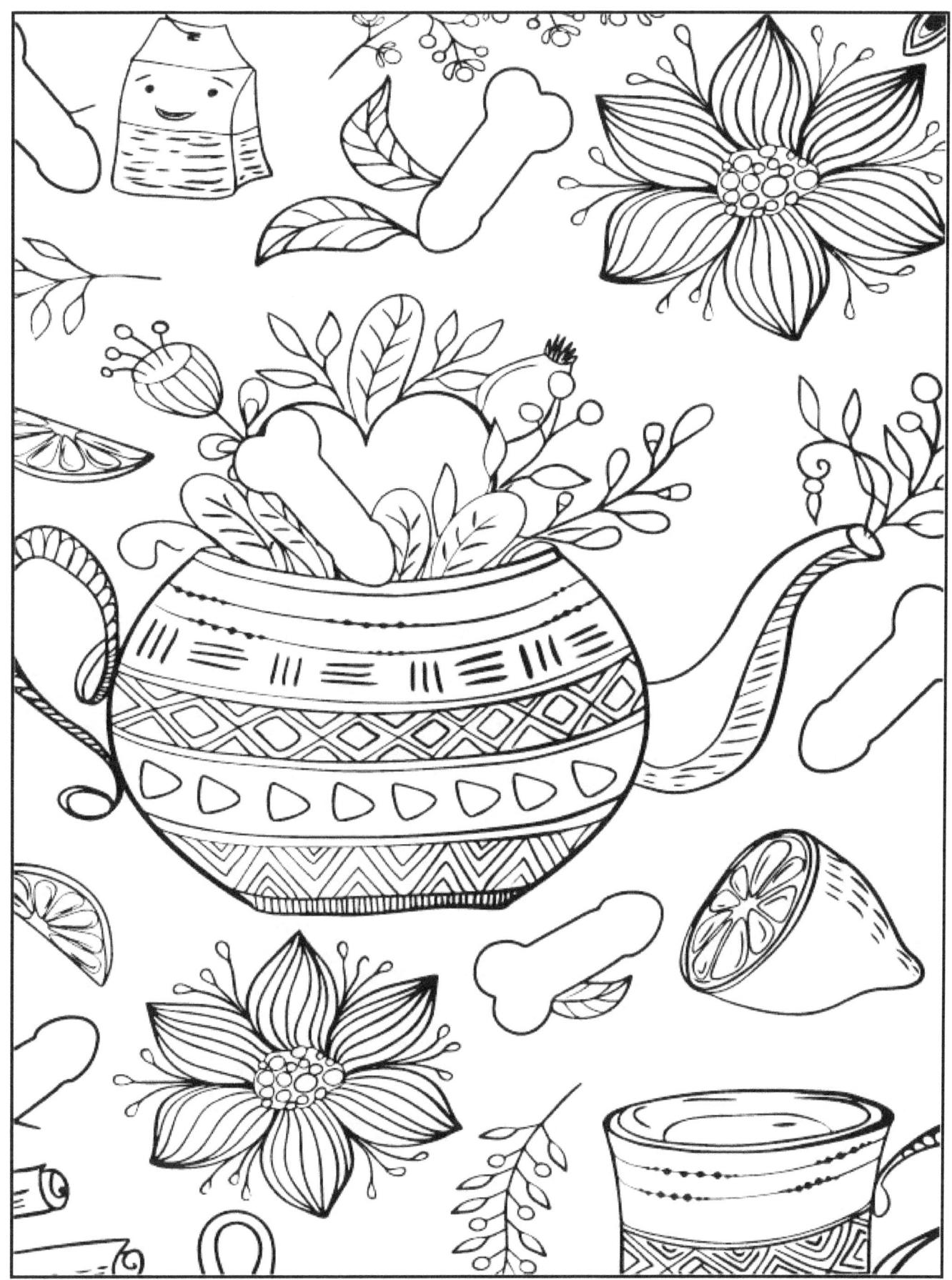

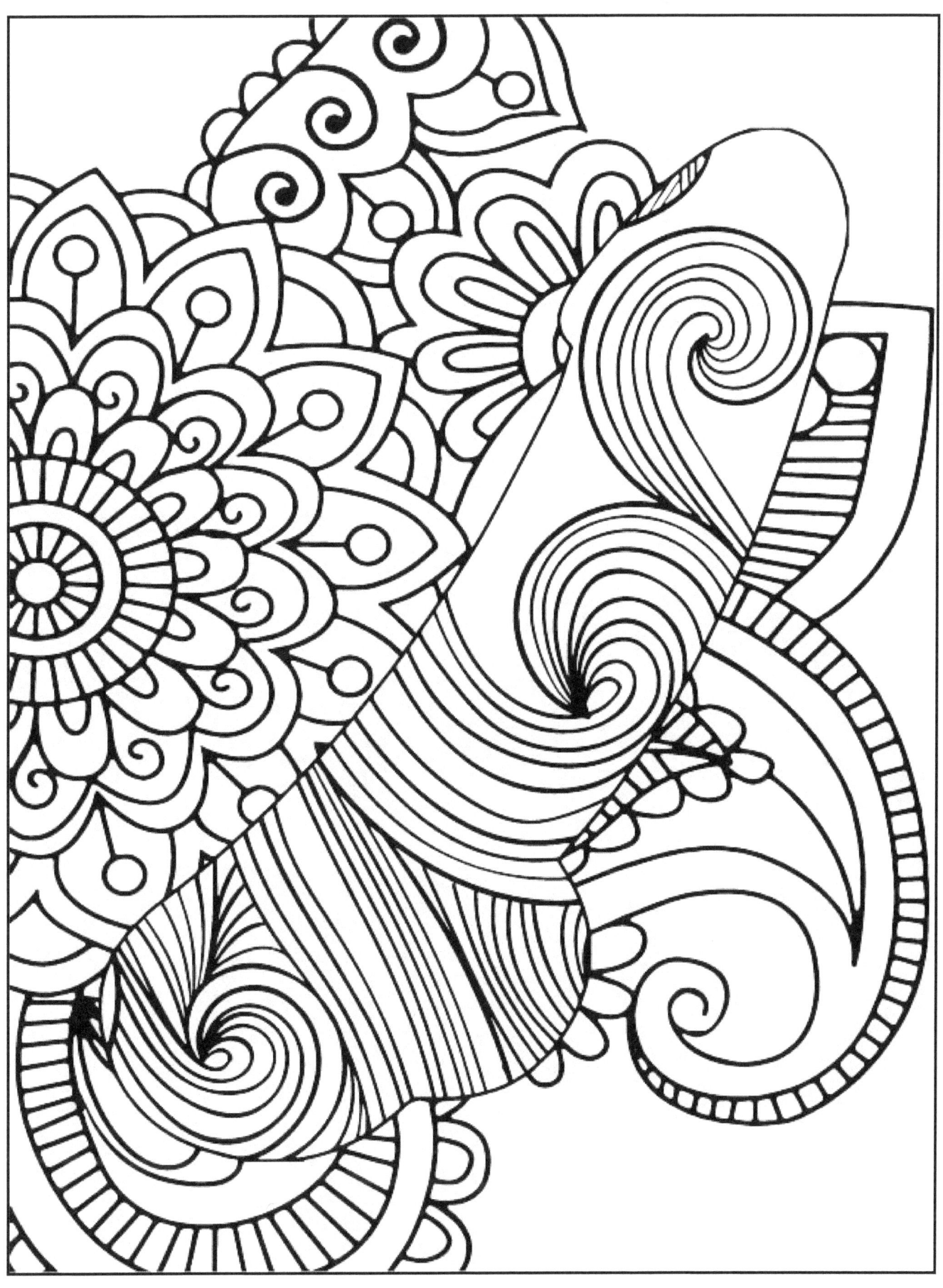

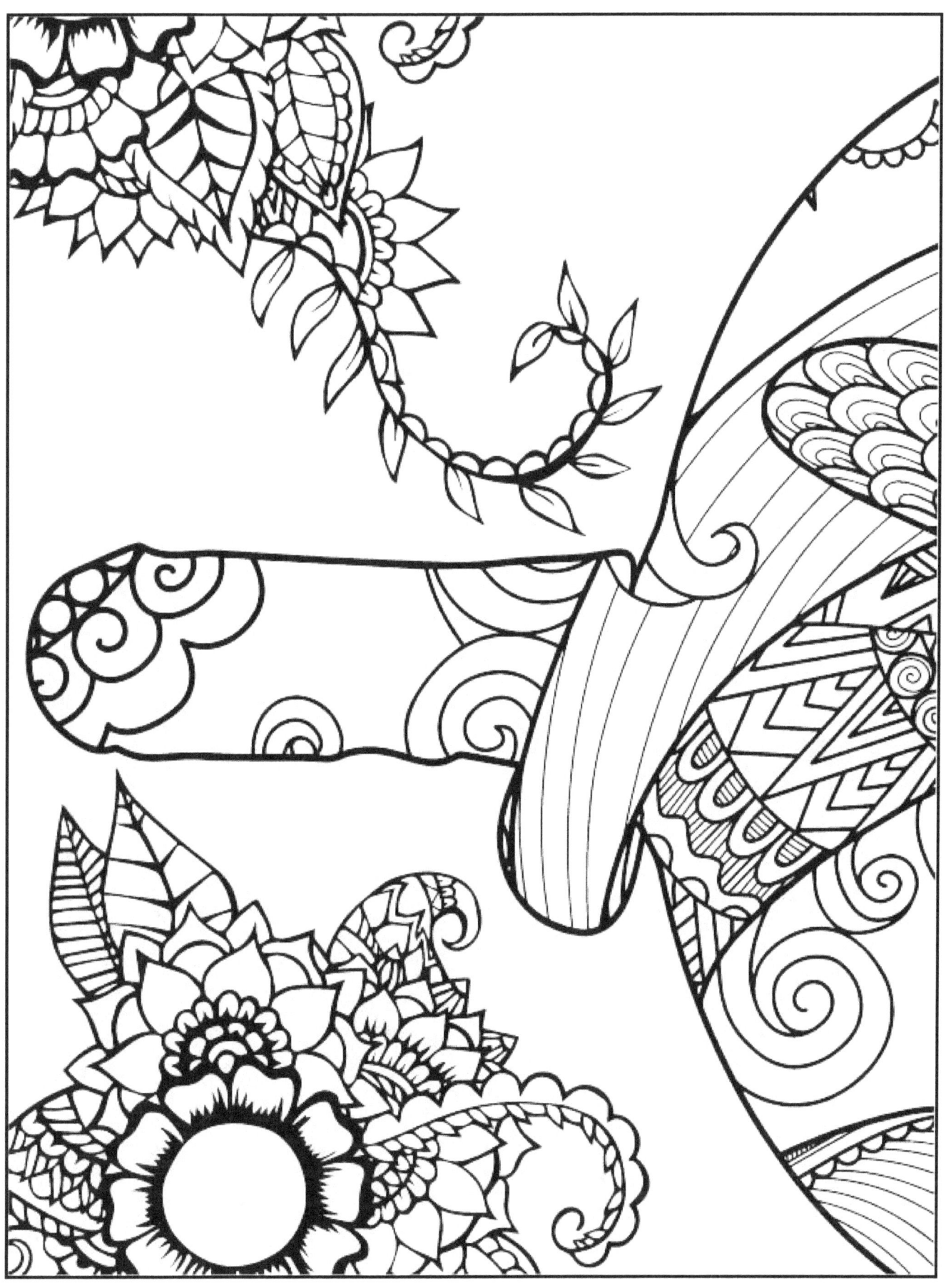

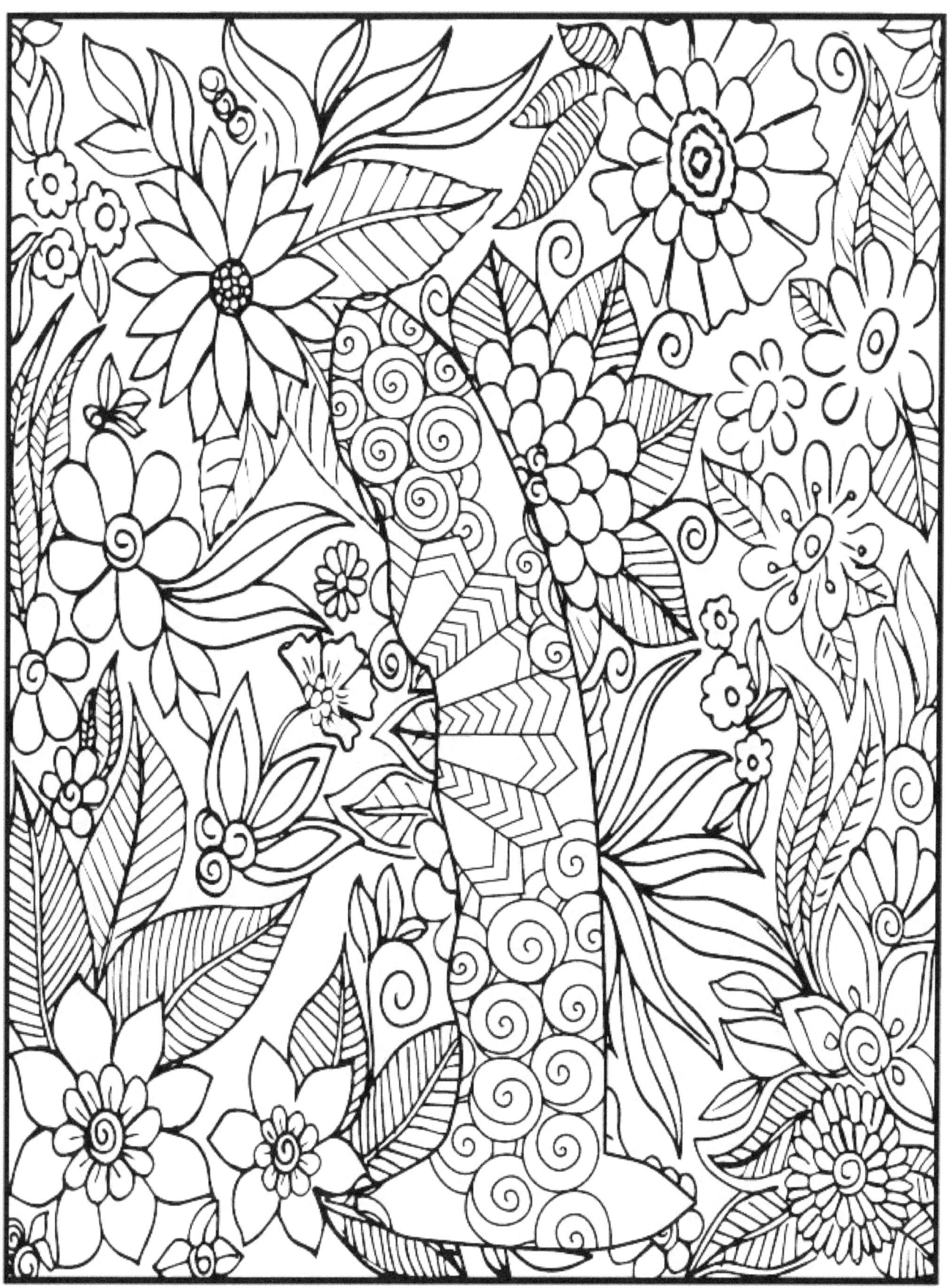

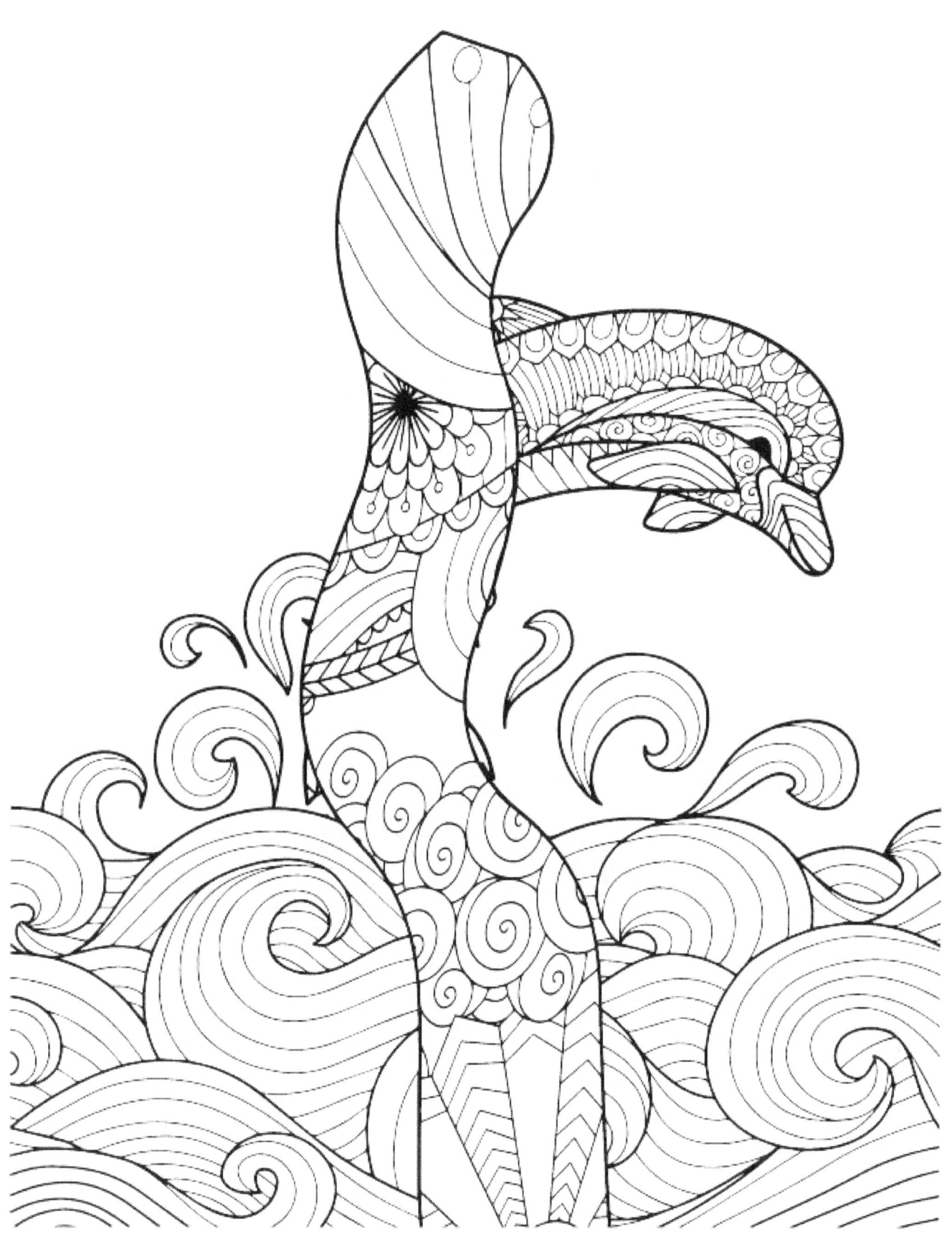

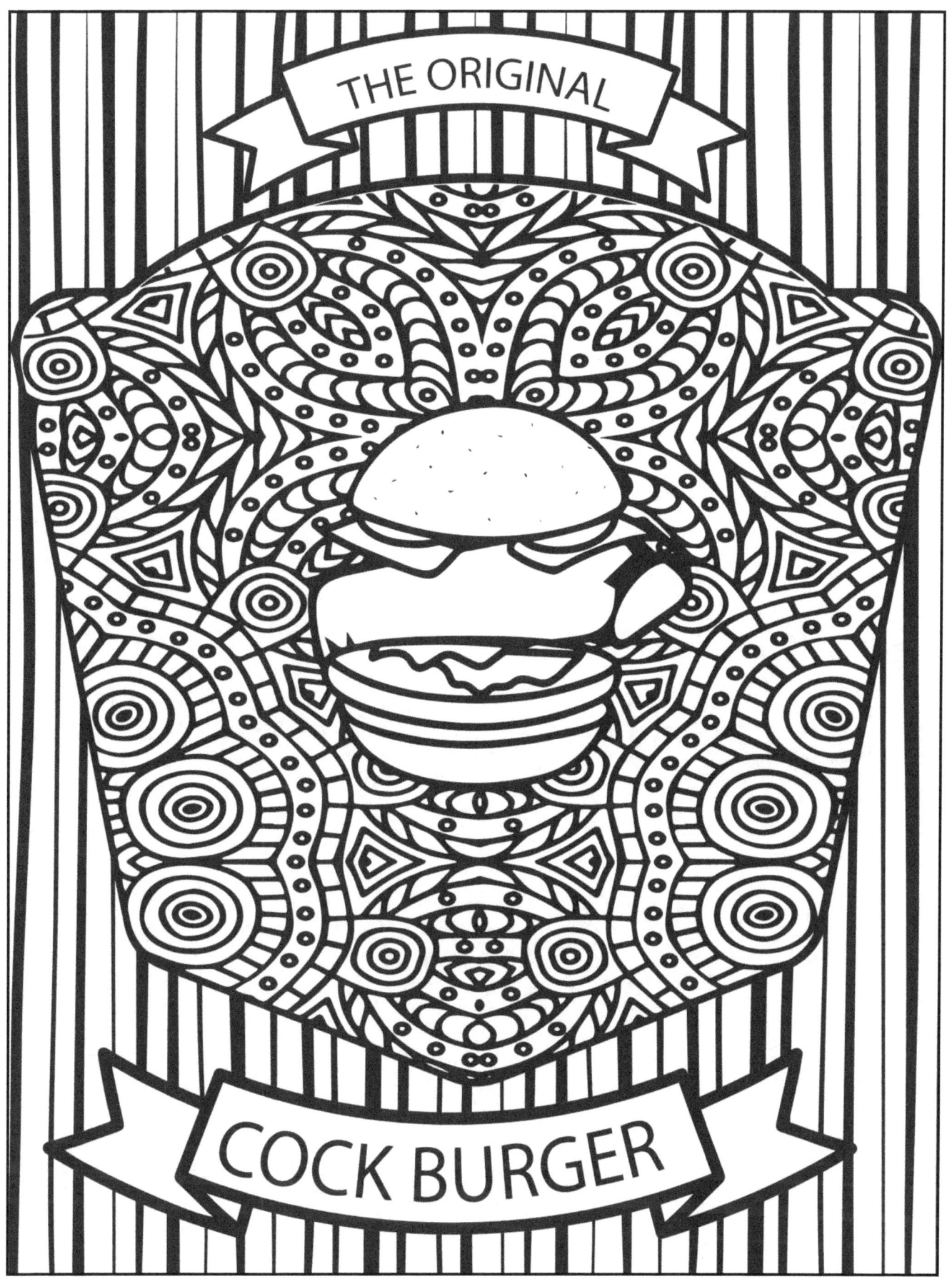

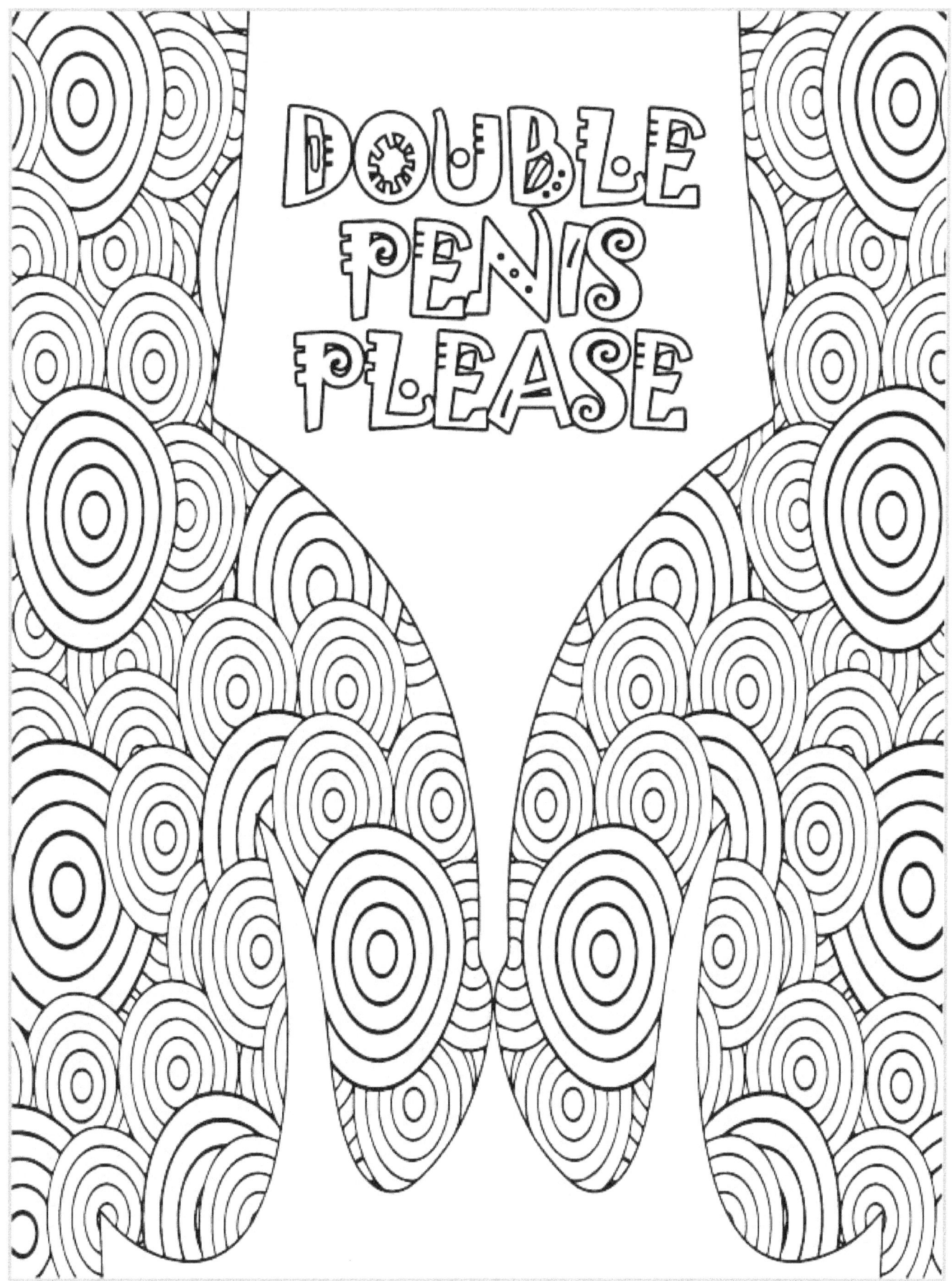

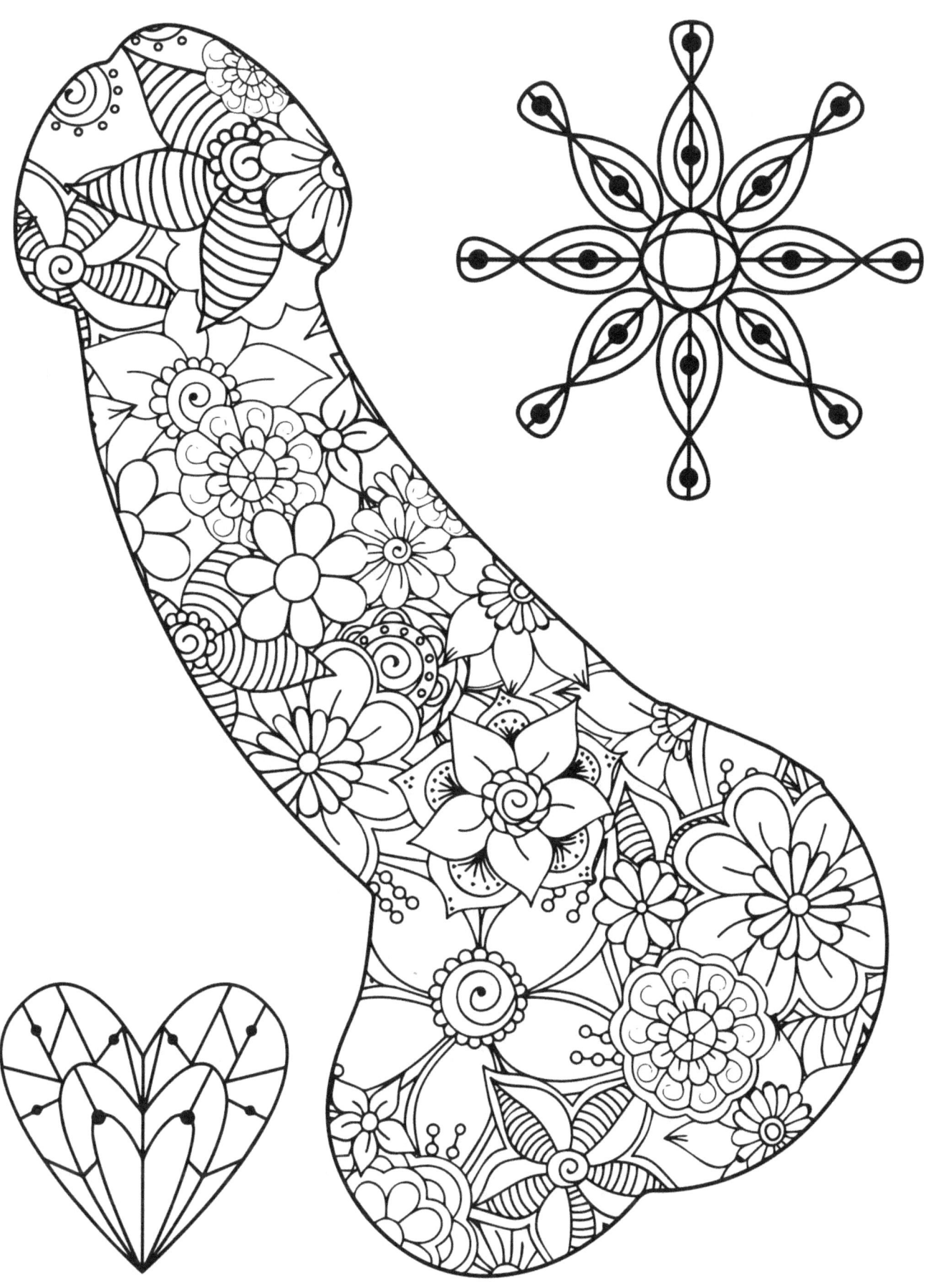

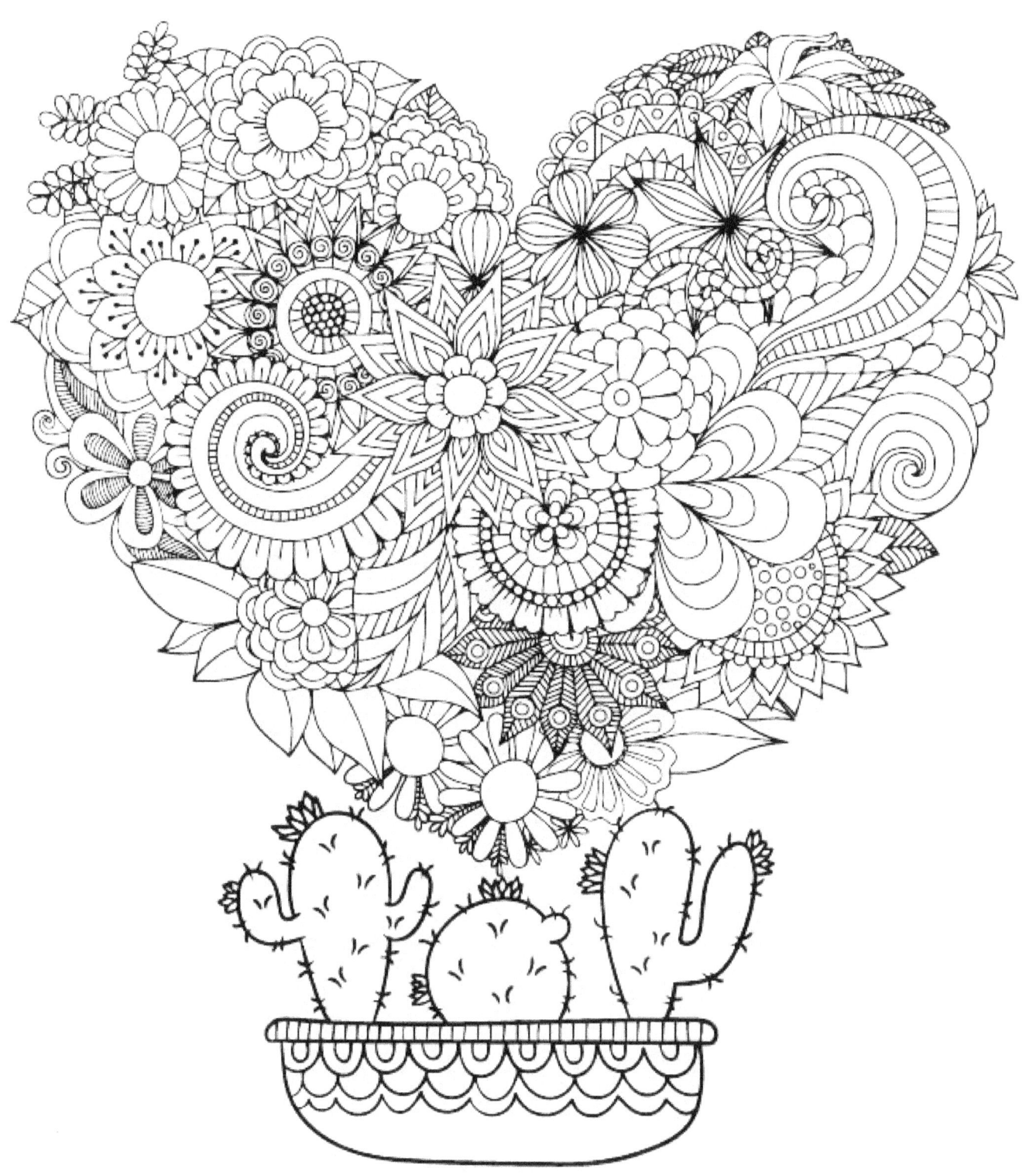

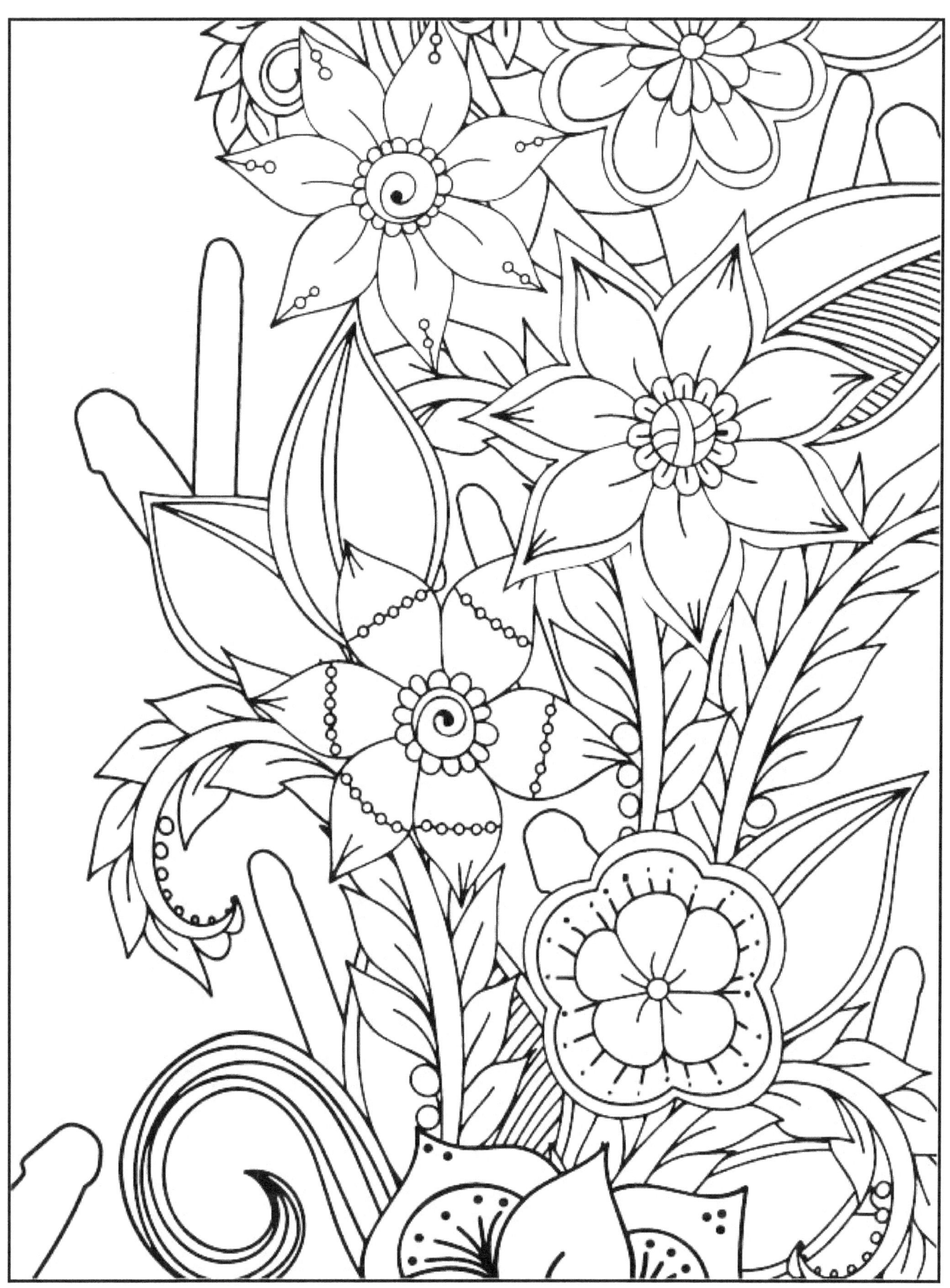

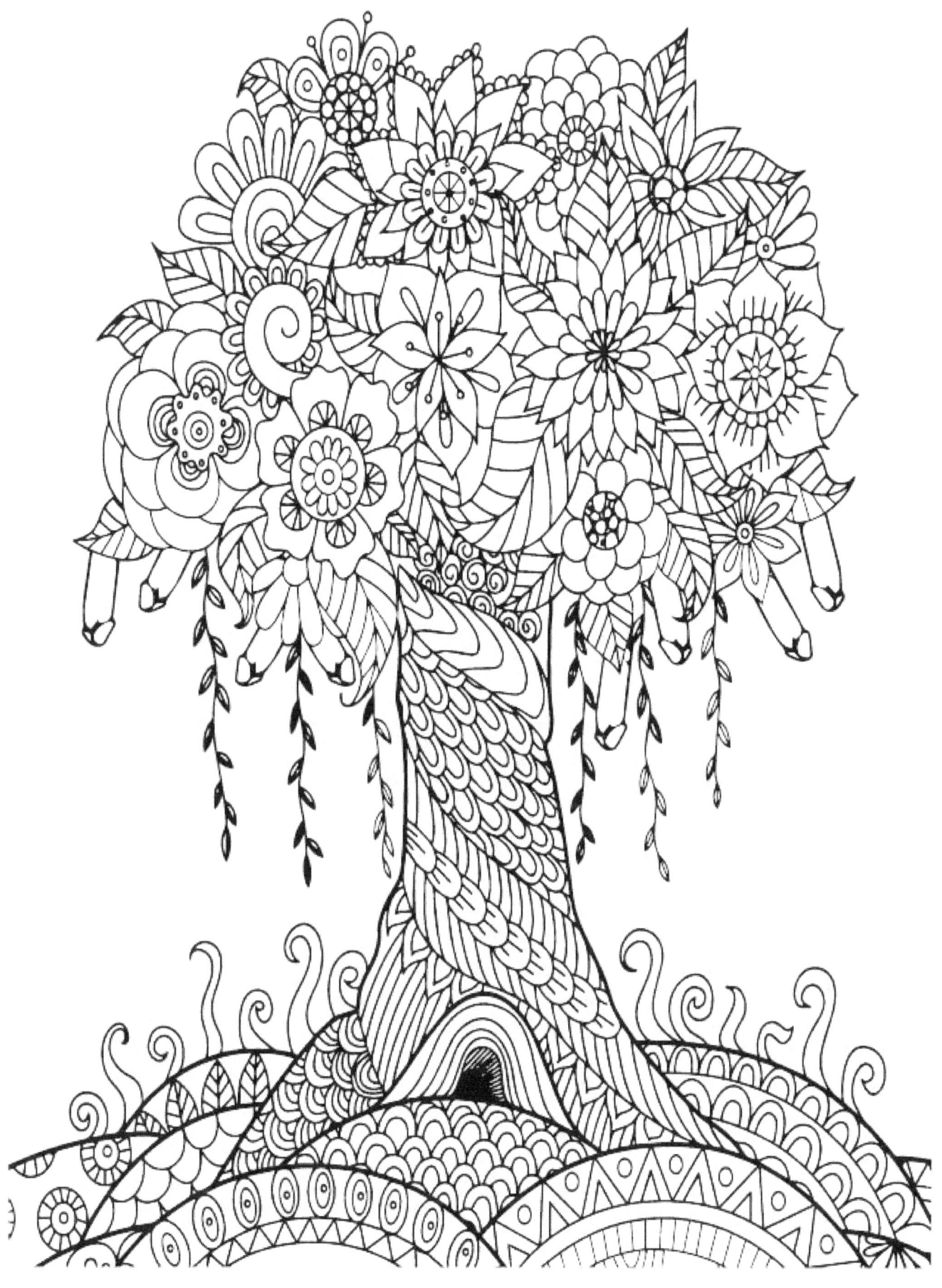

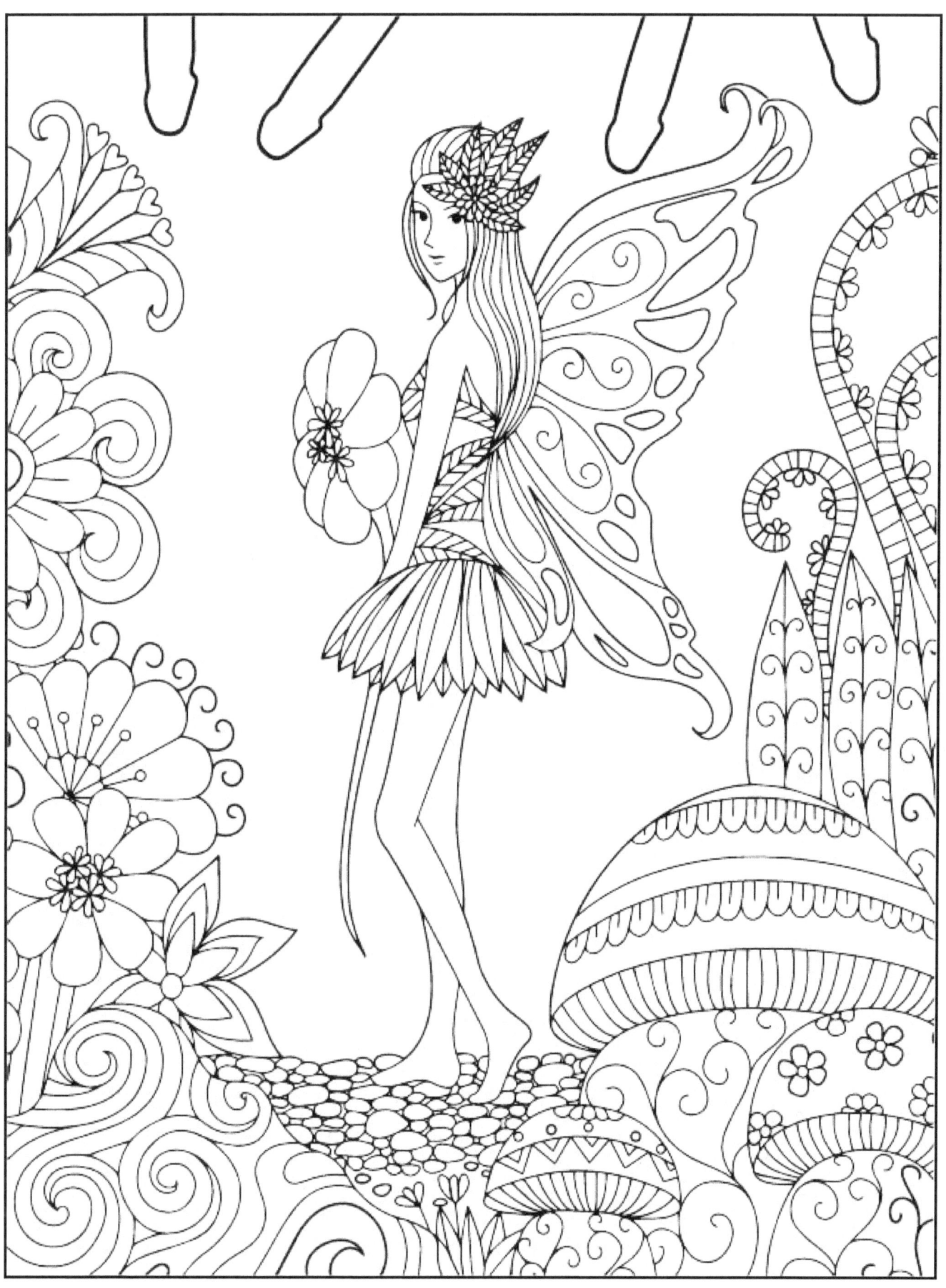

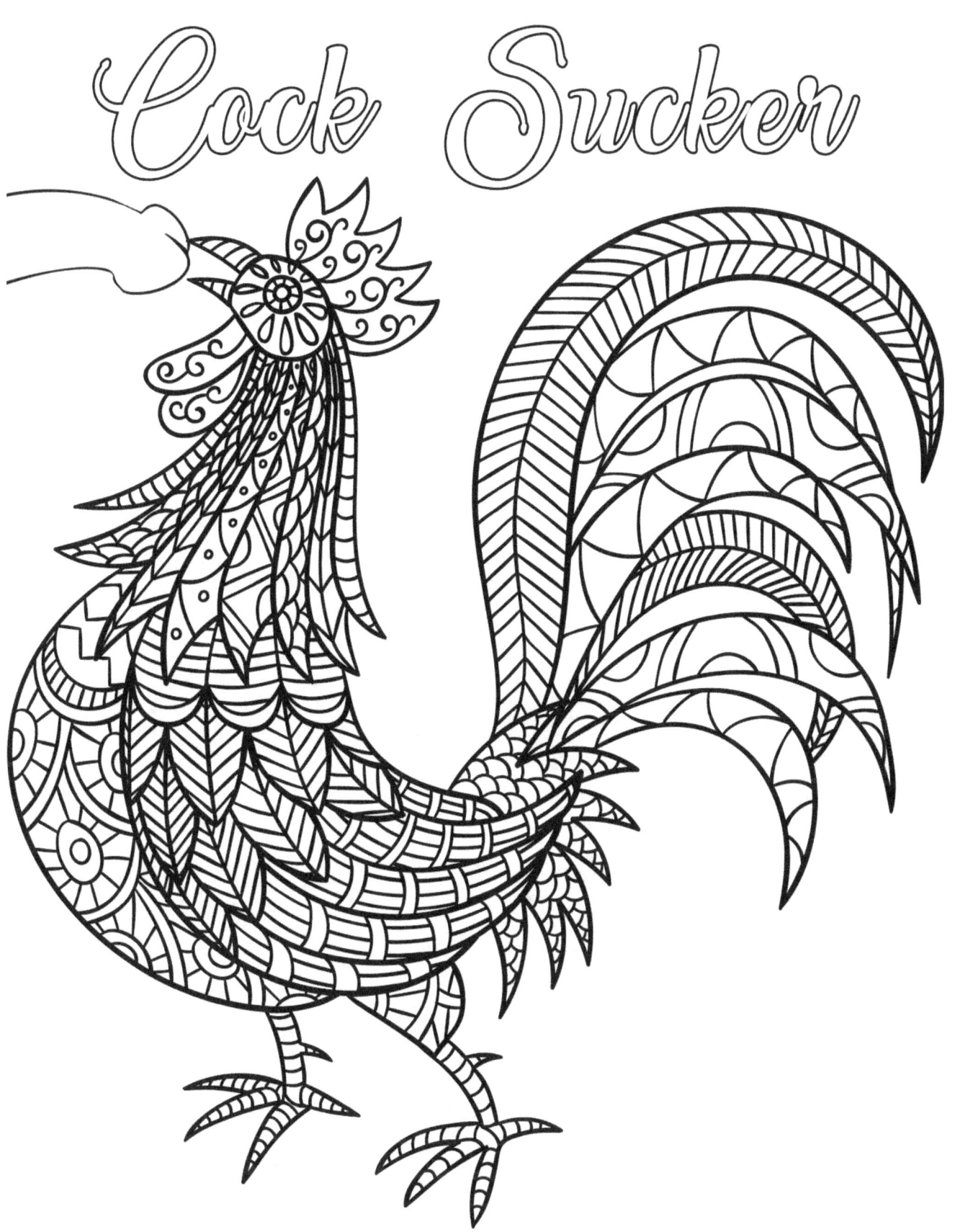

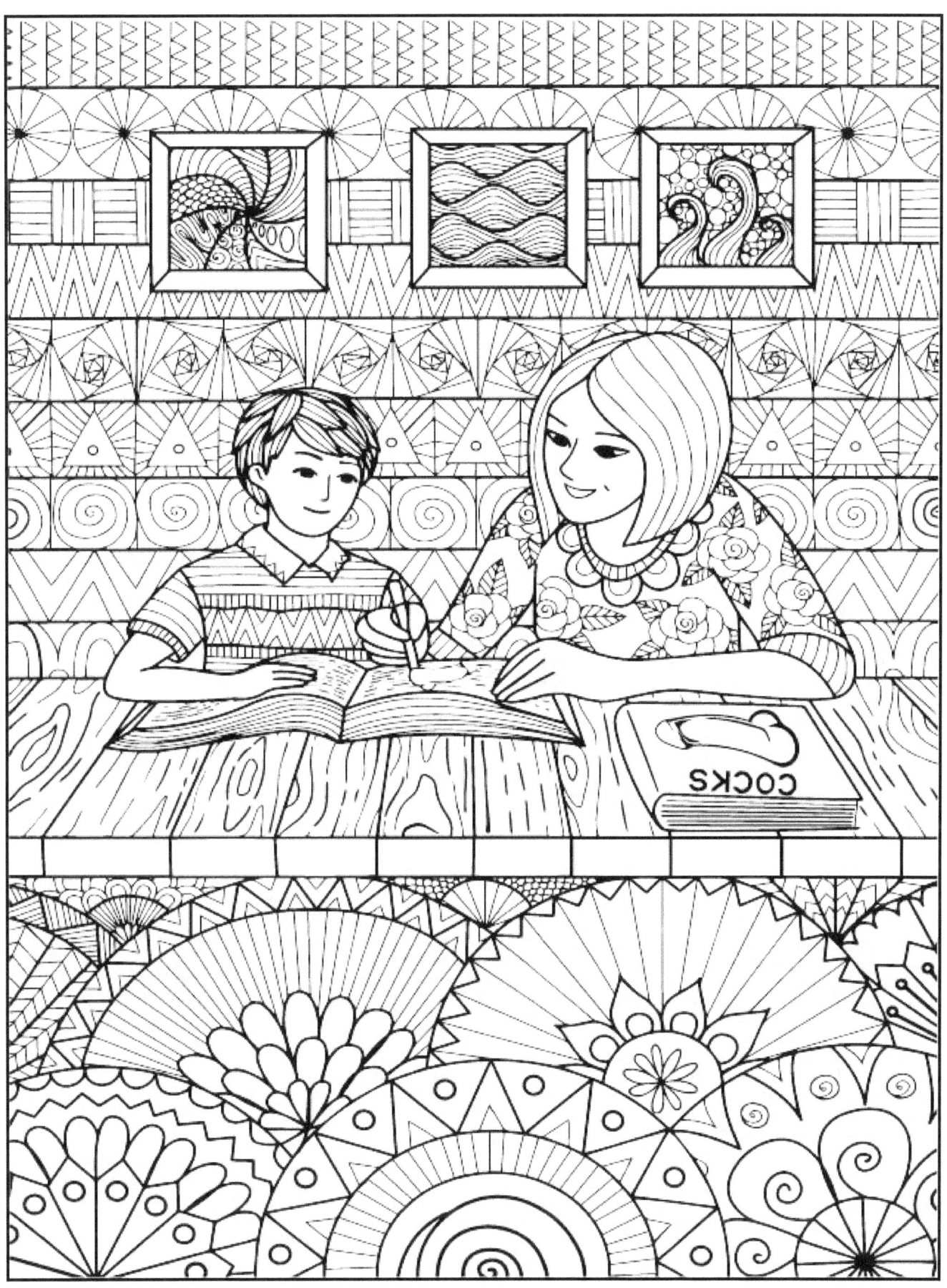

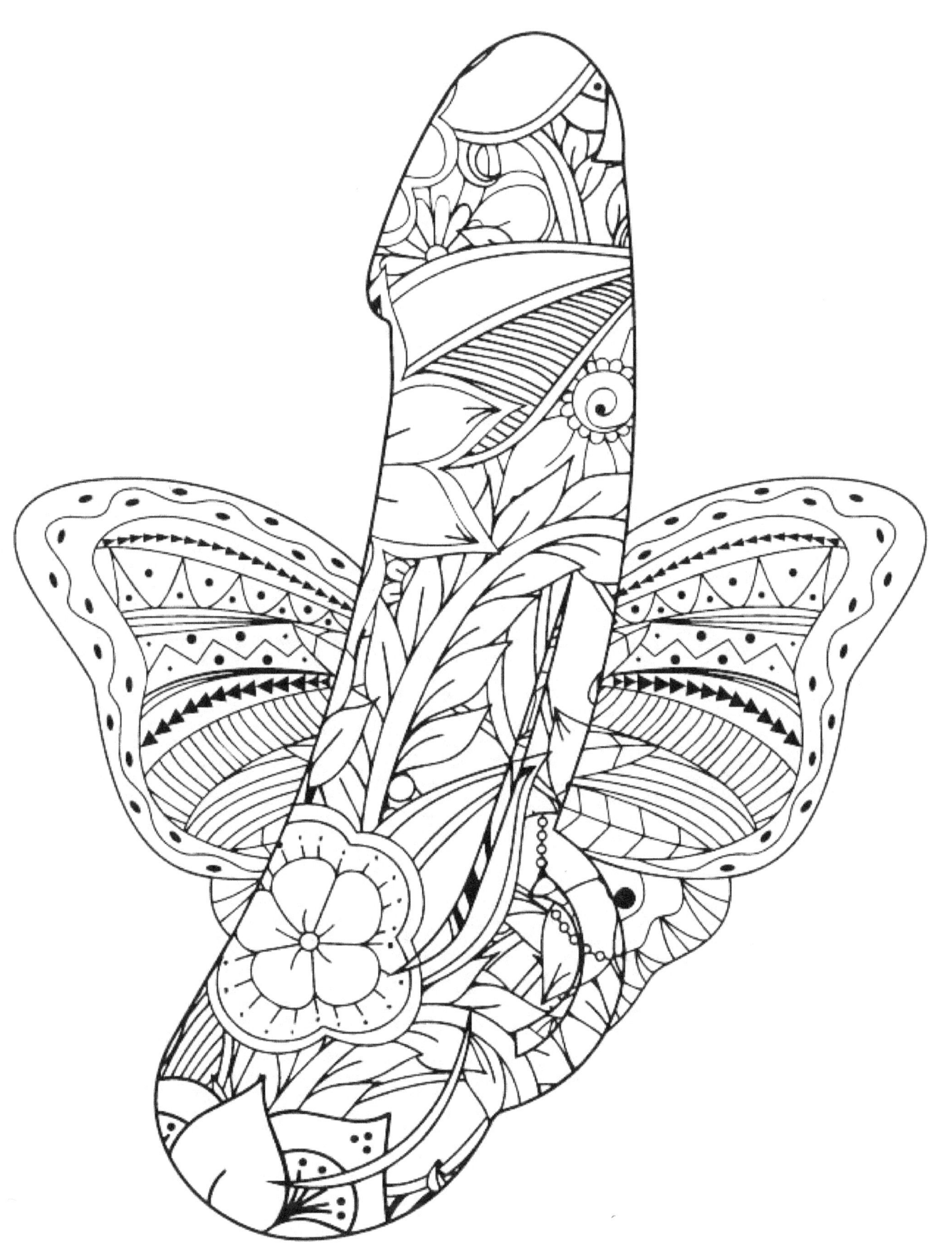

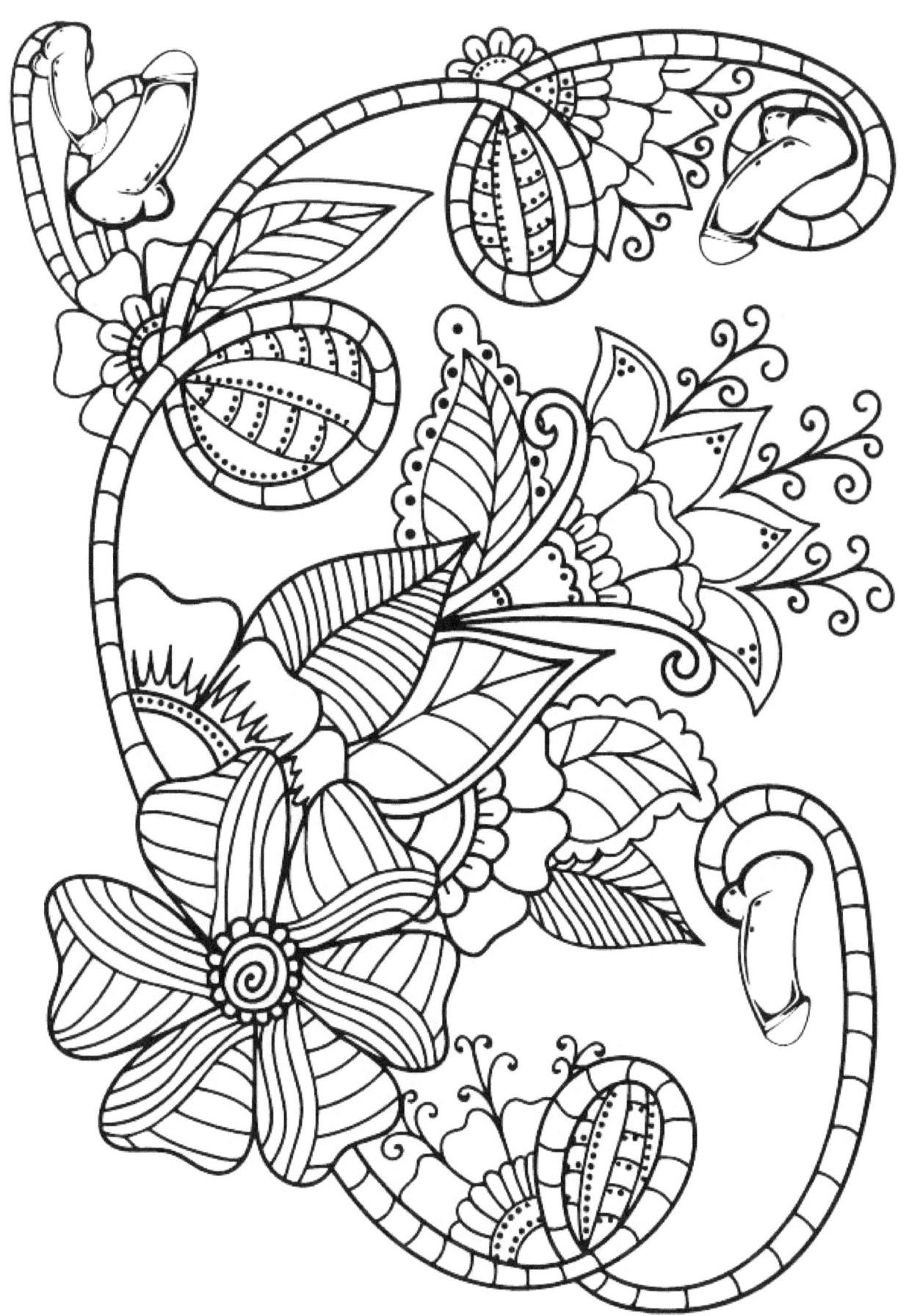

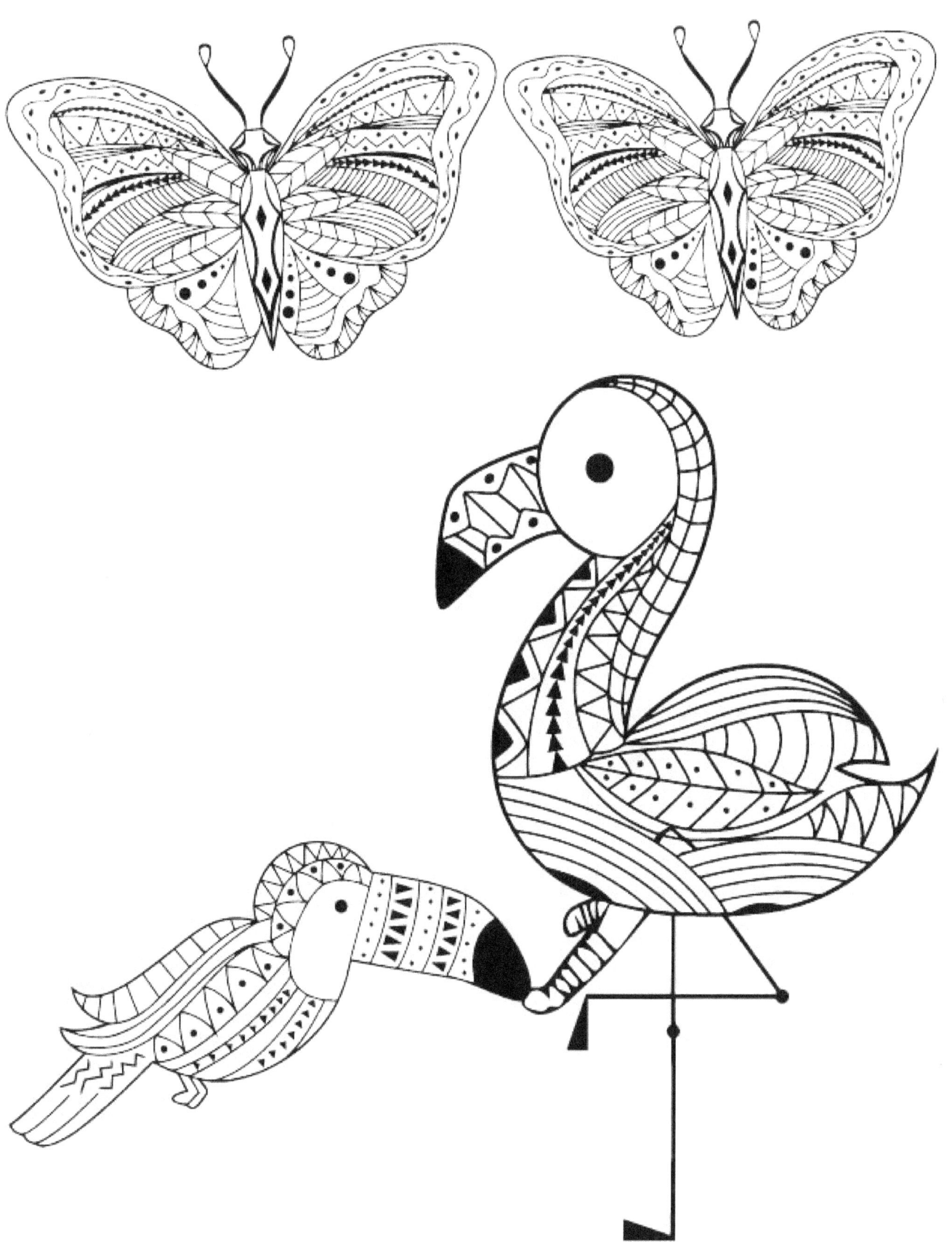

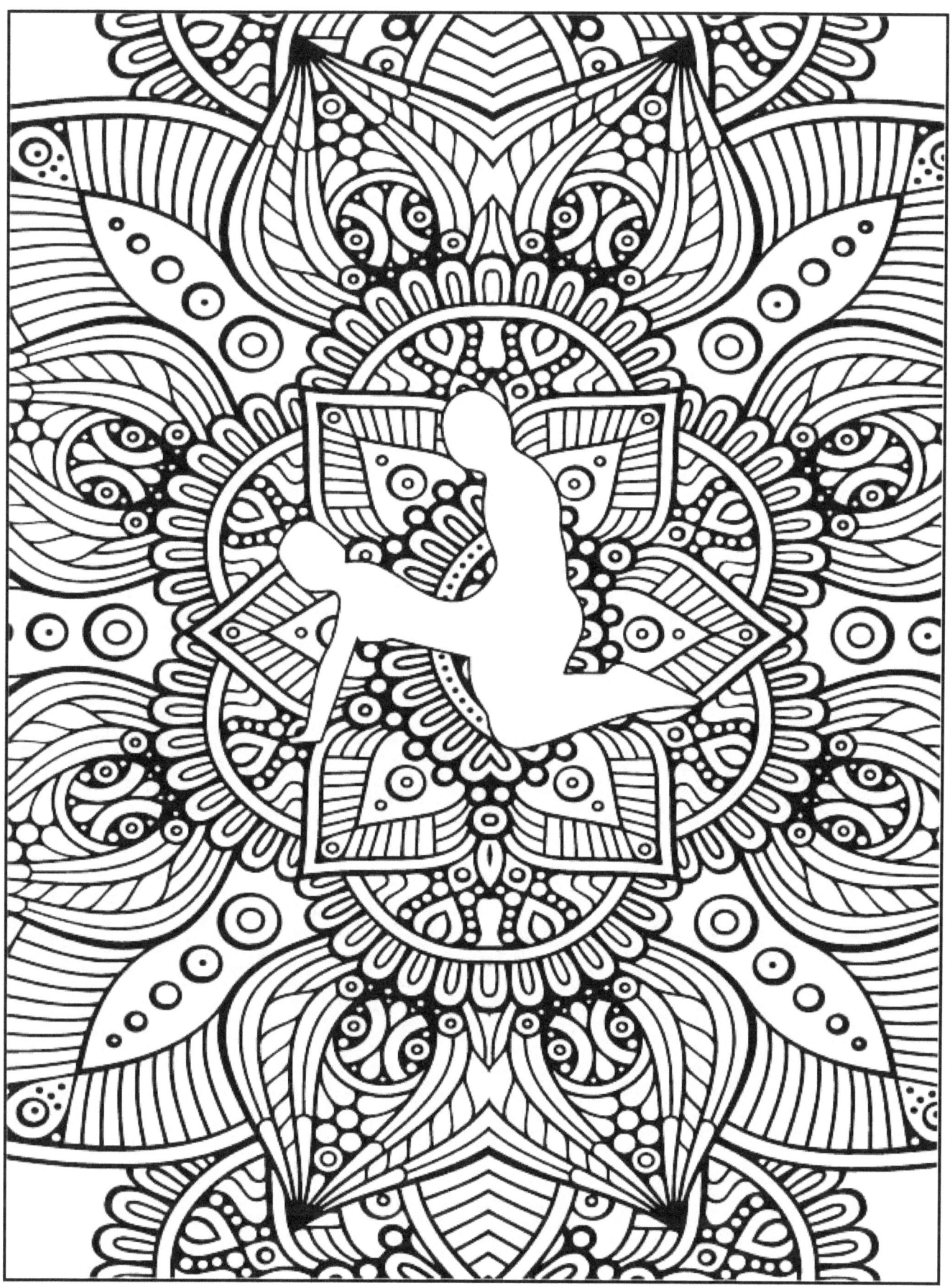

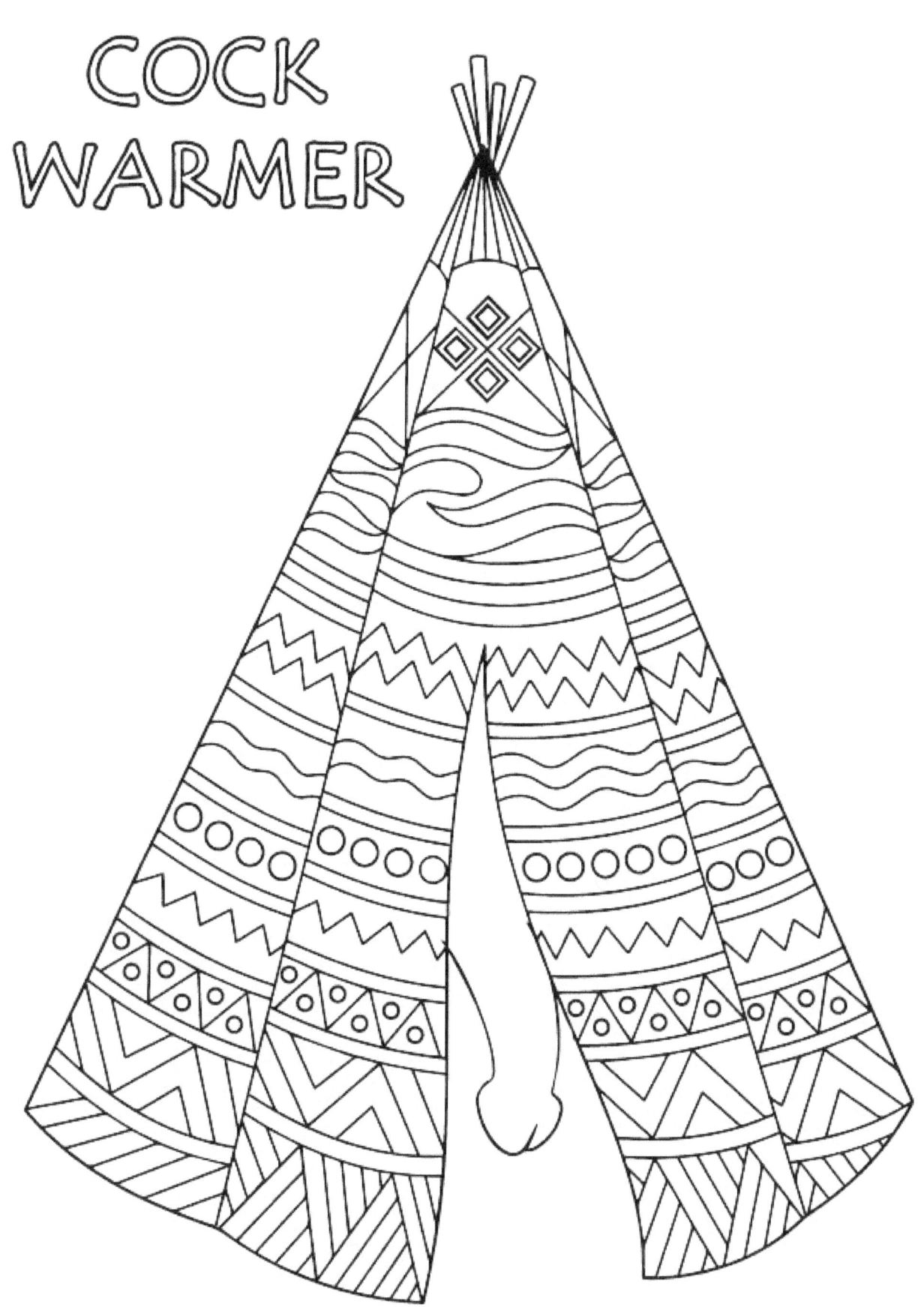

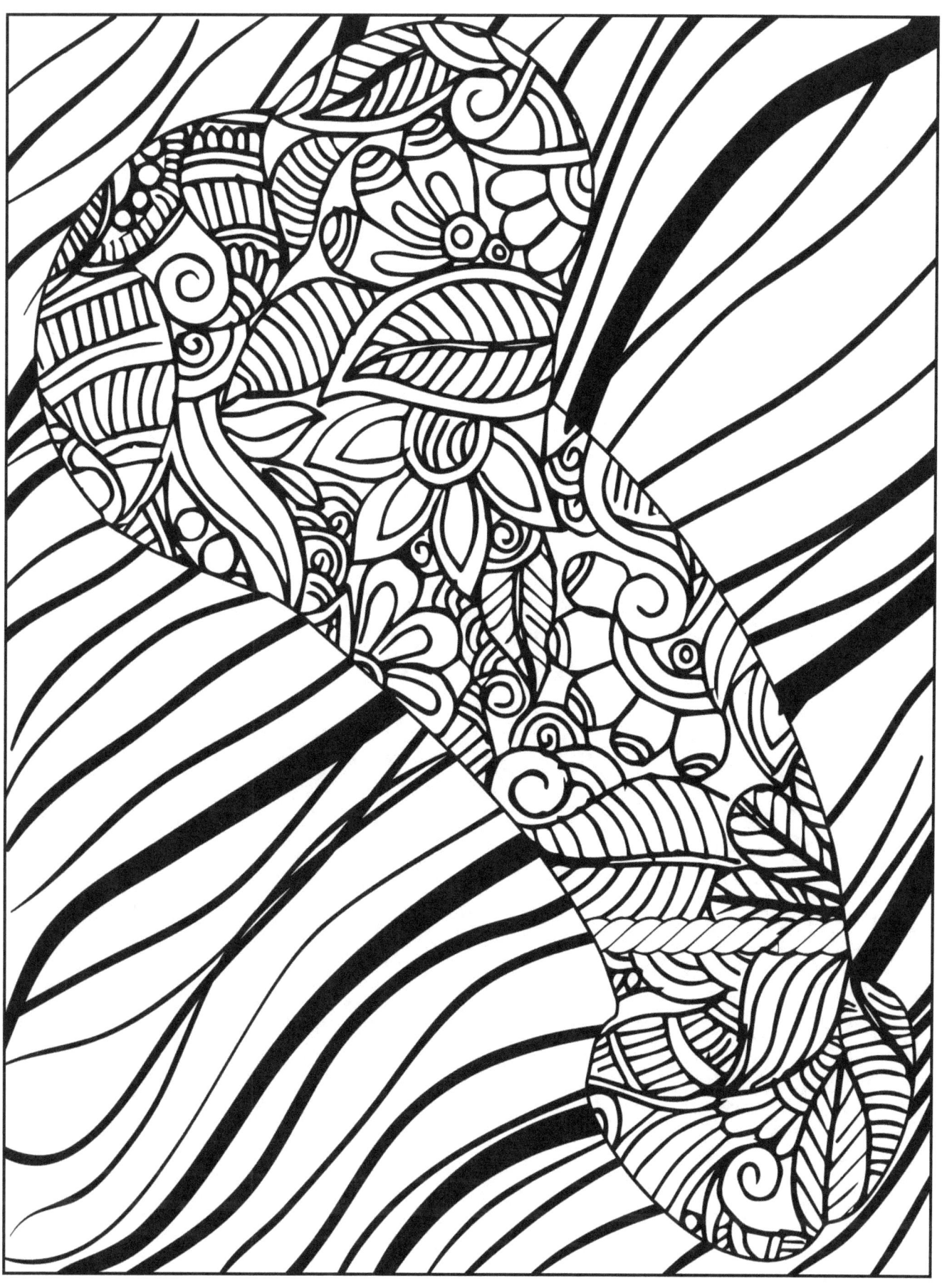

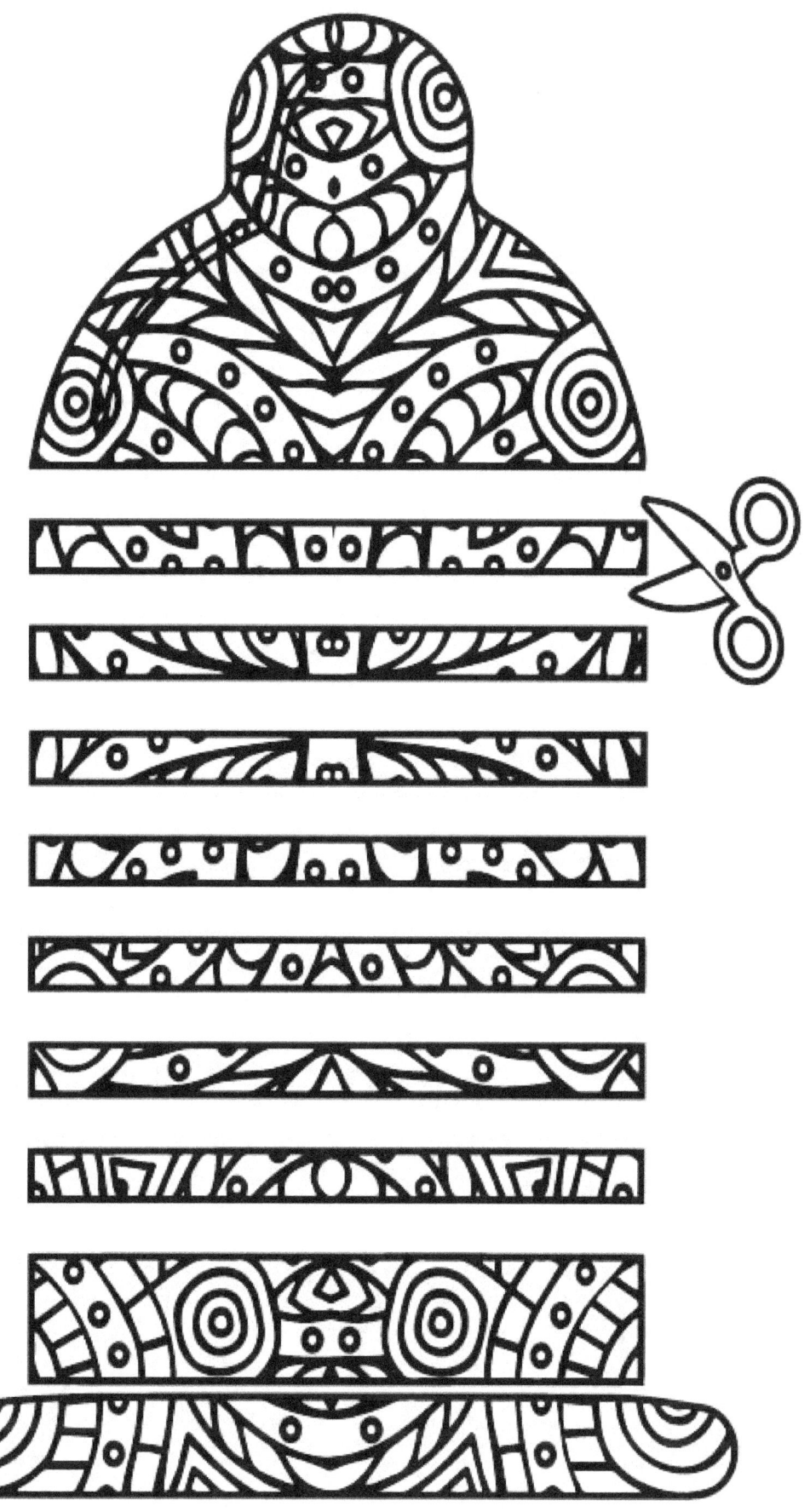

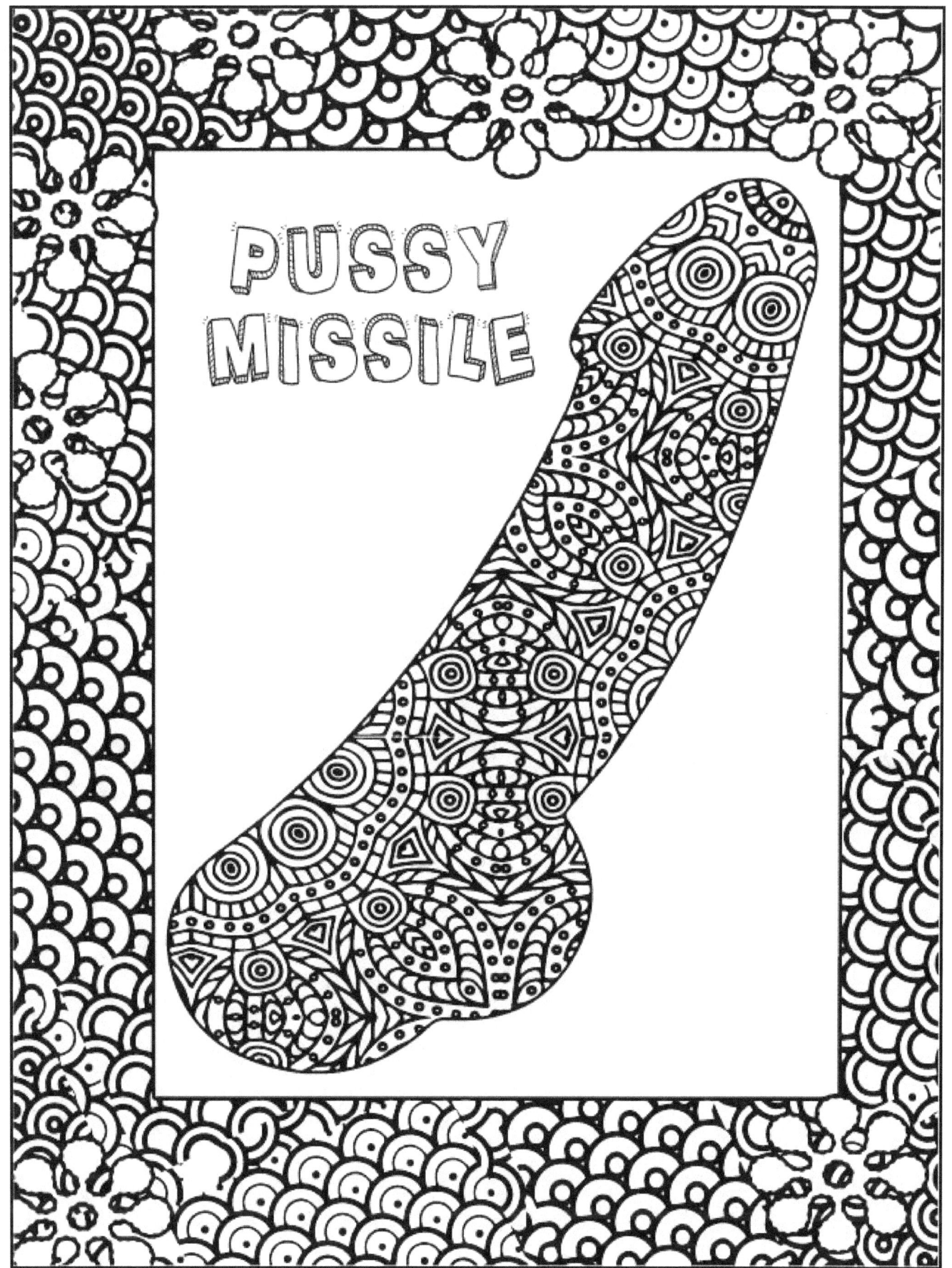

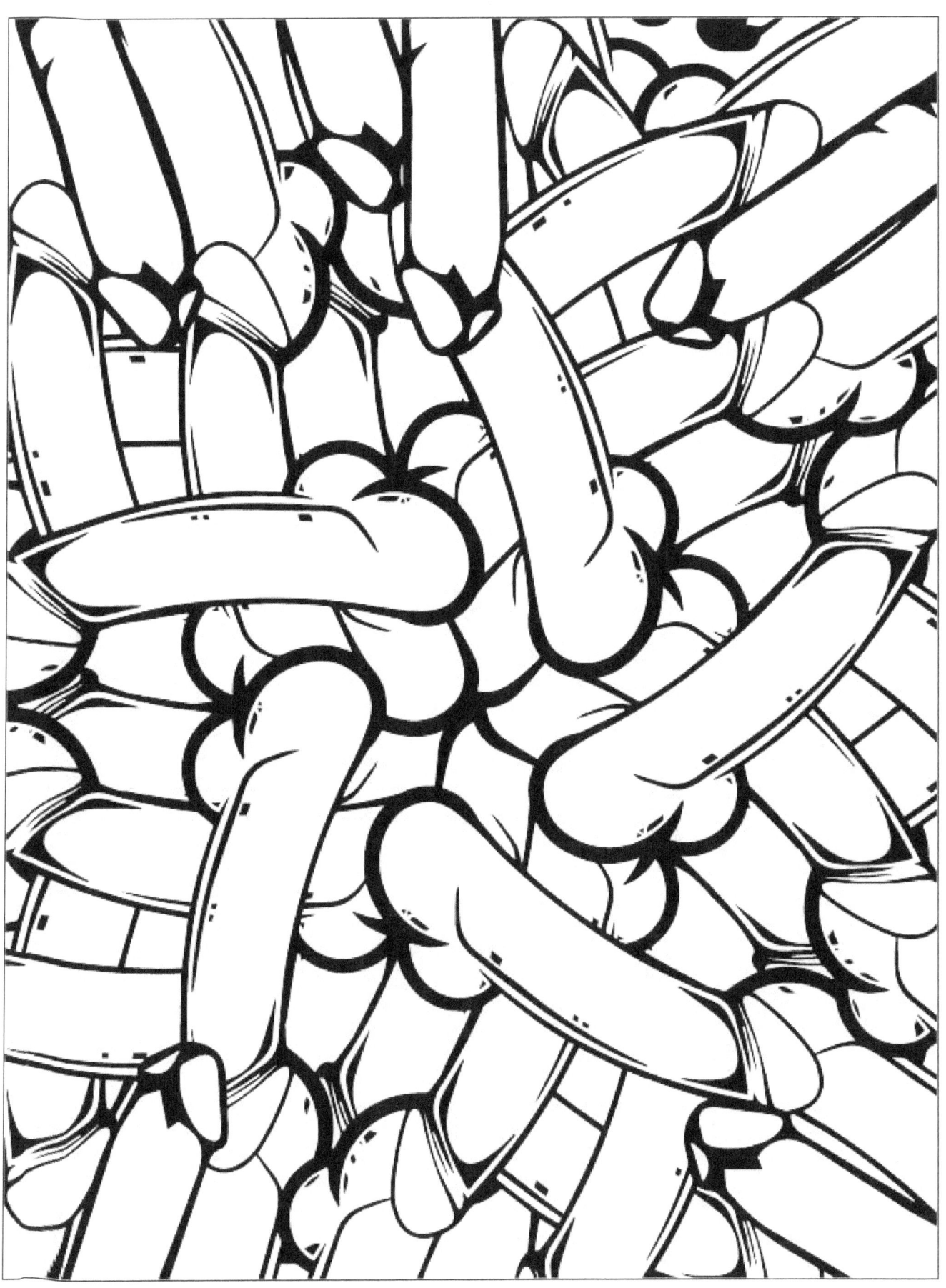

www.ingramcontent.com/pod-product-compliance
Lightning Source LLC
Chambersburg PA
CBHW081121240526
45470CB00019B/2838